PREPARING TO BEAR ARMS:

The Armorbearer's Guide to Making Your Pastor Look Good

By Delton Ellis

xulon PRESS

Preparing to Bear Arms
by Delton Ellis

Printed in the United States of America

ISBN 1-60034-573-5

www.xulonpress.com

DEDICATION

—◊◊◊—

This book is dedicated to:

Bishop Neil C. Ellis and First Lady Patrice Ellis

This book is dedicated to my Pastor, Bishop Neil C. Ellis and First Lady Patrice Ellis who have provided the opportunity for me to serve them for the past 10 years and to develop my gifts. Their high standards for service in Ministry has taught me how to serve with a Spirit of excellence and to impart such knowledge to those who serve with me.

I would also like to acknowledge the hard-working Servants at Mount Tabor Full Gospel Baptist Church whom I have had the good fortune to serve with for the past decade. Your tireless and committed service to the work of Ministry is an inspiration to me. I pray God's blessings on you continually.

FOREWORD

—◊◊◊—

The role of the Armor Bearer is without a doubt, becoming increasingly important for effective ministry in the 21st Century Church. As leaders of progressive, visionary, Kingdom ministries strive to accomplish the "God sized" mandates assigned to them, it is vitally important that they have the kind of support and assistance that Armor Bearers provide.

I do believe however, that there presently exists widespread confusion on the roles and responsibilities of Armor Bearers from both a biblical and practical perspective. I am therefore extremely delighted that Pastor Delton Ellis has decided to write on this all too important topic; thereby utilizing and sharing with others years of insight and information gained from over a decade of "on the job training" and spiritual processing in his capacity as an excellent armor bearer to me.

This is sure to be a powerful, practical, exhaustive and tremendously useful tool not only for Armor Bearers in terms of helping to equip them for the work of Ministry, but it will also serve as a great source of information for leaders as it provides them with a measuring tool to determine what to look for in choosing Armor Bearers.

I praise God for the fact that I can truly say that Pastor Ellis has proven to be a tremendous blessing to me and to the Mount Tabor ministry and he exemplifies and embodies what Biblical Armor Bearing is all about.

I congratulate him on this work and assure you, that you and your ministry will be blessed by the information contained herein and further by the application of it.

TO GOD BE ALL THE GLORY!

Bishop Neil C. Ellis, C.M.G., D.D., J.P.
Senior Pastor, Mount Tabor Full Gospel Baptist Church
Nassau, Bahamas

TABLE OF CONTENTS

—𝔪—

INTRODUCTION

—∿∿—

I have been involved in church ministry for almost 20 years, and during this time I have seen a whole lot of things. As I endeavor to fulfill the mandate that God has given me to train and prepare ministry workers to serve in their local congregations, I felt compelled to write a book specifically for those who work in close proximity to and in close contact with the senior pastor. I believe that this is an area of ministry that has been grossly misused and at times misunderstood. If you have this book in your hands, it means one of two things; either you have been chosen by your pastor to be an Armorbearer, or you want to learn more about the duties of an Armorbearer. In either case, you are to be commended for the desire to learn and to know more. This is a good starting point.

The purpose of this book is to prepare Armorbearers for WHAT they should do, WHEN they should do it and HOW it should be done. I know that this book will be a blessing to Armorbearers and senior pastors alike because it is something from which they both will benefit. The Armorbearer who knows what to do and does it well will greatly lighten the load of the one he serves. Most senior pastors know what they want and what they need in an Armorbearer, but few of them have the time, energy or focus to spend time training them. I have come to discover that not every person is able to learn "on-the-job" and because of this, senior pastors become easily frustrated with those who serve closest to them. Some pastors believe (sometimes mistakenly) that the Armorbearer should "know" what to do and when to do it, and that such responsibility does not warrant direction or conversation. The Armorbearer on the other hand is doing the best he can and even with the best of intentions, he is not as much help as he is trying to be. This book is intended to help Armorbearers and those who serve to bridge this gap.

Even though many people want to serve as Armorbearers, they do not fully understand what the position entails. In fact, some who serve in this office today do not really understand it. In the distance, it looks glamorous and perhaps worthy to be sought after, but on close examination and thorough review, you will come to discover that this post is really for the person who has a spiritual connection with his pastor first and foremost. If your motivation for seeking this place of ministry is to get close to the senior pastor or to be associated with the "big names" in international ecclesia, you are not ready for this assignment. Being an Armorbearer is a selfless position. By that I mean that you have to be more concerned for the one you serve than for yourself. You cannot put your feelings or your ambitions and desires above the act of serving your pastor. I know this is difficult, but this is what is required. Selfish people will never make good Armorbearers.

If you read the Table of Contents of this book you will note that every chapter speaks about "Preparation." An Armorbearer is always preparing for something, preparing for someone or preparing himself to be used by God. As you read this book, you will note further that an Armorbearer is never off duty. His work is never done. There is always some aspect of his service or his character and personality that needs to be worked on. There is always another situation that needs to be resolved and another matter to keep in prayer before God. In this book, Armorbearers of the Bible are used as case studies to examine the characteristics and functions that can be extracted and used by those who work with the senior pastor today. If you understand these principles and apply them to your life and service, I know that you will be a successful Armorbearer. May God bless you as you endeavor to fulfill his call on your life to serve your senior pastor.

CHAPTER ONE

PREPARING TO BEAR ARMS

—⟋⟍—

"The preparations of the heart belong to man but the answer of the tongue is from the LORD."

Proverbs 16:1

Serving as an Armorbearer requires preparation. Perhaps 80 percent of what you do as a helper is concerned with preparation. Making sure that you have prepared yourself to serve, making sure that you have made preparations for your pastor, making sure that the atmosphere is prepared and that it is conducive for the ministry of your pastor, and finally, making sure that those who will receive the ministry of your pastor have made adequate preparations for his arrival and for his service. In order to prepare yourself to serve as an Armorbearer, it is important to know who or what is an Armorbearer.

<u>WHAT IS AN ARMORBEARER?</u>

The word *Armorbearer* is translated from two Hebrew words. The first word is **'NASA'** which means to lift, to accept, advance, bear up, hold up, help, raise, respect, or to stir up. The second word is **'KEL-EE'** which comes from the root word **KALAH** meaning to end or to fulfill, to bring to pass or to complete. Putting these terms together, we arrive at the concept of the term "Armorbearer" that will be discussed throughout the book. **An Armorbearer is a person who walks with, holds up and protects the senior pastor and does what is necessary to help him fulfill and bring to pass his God-given vision.**

Your senior pastor has been anointed to give vision and leadership for the ministry and to the people who in turn will build the Kingdom of God. The pastor's ministry is to set up, build, encourage, motivate, instruct, convert and shepherd the multitudes that God has placed in his church. Even though pastors have an awesome responsibility in fulfilling the call of God on their lives, God does not expect them to do it alone. According to Habakkuk 2:2, when the pastor receives a vision from God, they are to write it and make it plain so that those who read it can run it. That includes those who lift up and support the pastor – Armorbearers. Let's look at Exodus 18:13-18:

*And so it was, on the next day, that Moses sat to judge the people; and the people stood before Moses from morning until evening. So when Moses' father-in-law saw all that he did for the people, he said, "What is this thing that you are doing for the people? Why do you alone sit, and all the people stand before you from morning until evening? And Moses said to his father-in-law, "Because the people come to me to inquire of God." When they have a difficulty, they come to me, and I judge between one and another; and I make known the statutes of God and His laws. So Moses' father-in-law said to him, "The thing that you do is not good. Both you and these people who are with you will surely wear yourselves out. **For*** *this thing is too much for you; you are not able to perform it by yourself."*

It was never the plan of God that those who occupy the five–fold ministry offices do all the work of the ministry. Even if it were possible, it is not desirable because there is only so much one person can do. Moses' father-in-law saw this and admonished him to get others to help. This is the primary reason for Armorbearers. They are to help, support and lift up their pastors as they complete the work of ministry that God has assigned to them. That is the definition of the term in its simplest form.

THE ROLE AND FUNCTION OF THE ARMORBEARER

The role of the Armorbearer is to help the pastor's vision come alive by supporting and assisting him. The term Armorbearer is not an office or title; it is a **responsibility**. It is not an adjective describing an office, but it is a verb to denote "doing" something. Armorbearers *lift up* and *support* the pastor.

From the Scriptures, we learn the following things about Armorbearers;

❖ An Armorbearer is defined in Scripture as one who bears arms. It is the person who carries the armor of a king, commander-in-chief, captain or other high-ranking official.

❖ Armorbearers were prepared to give their lives in order to defend and protect the life of the ones they served.

❖ The primary responsibility of the Armorbearer is to protect his assignee during battle. His focus is singular—it is to the person to whom he has been assigned and no one else, unless he has been so designated.

❖ Armorbearers were faithful, committed and present until the death of their leaders.

There are other things we will note about those who served as Armorbearers. Some were not prepared, some did not protect and some of them betrayed their leaders. I believe all of them had good intentions, but I believe some of them became victims of their circumstances because they were not prepared for all of the demands of this office. I want to help you so that you do not become a victim of circumstance and so that you will not fall under the heavy weight of this responsibility to serve your pastor directly. It may not be easy but it is possible, and if you are committed to it, you will achieve it. When you were chosen to be an Armorbearer, I know that you were honored! You should be. It is an appointment that should be esteemed very highly, but the real question is, "Are you ready for your assignment?"

THE CHARACTER OF AN ARMORBEARER

I am the last of ten children, and even though my family was a big one, my mother and father have traveled all over the world. Not because they were rich, but because of my father's character and integrity. I believe you know the saying, "Manners, respect and character will take you through the world" and it certainly did for my parents. Today, these are some of the most important characteristics Armorbearers can possess as they travel around the world with their pastors. When you serve as an Armorbearer, your character is just as important as your service.

The issue of character addresses the following questions: What kind of person are you? How are you dressed? How do you talk? What do you talk about? How do you behave when you are not serving? What kind of employee are you on your job? How important is your pastor to you? Can you be trusted to bear arms or should your pastor fear that you will use those protective weapons against him? These questions must be answered because they will have a significant impact on your ability to serve as an Armorbearer. A façade will only hold up for so long and then the real you will come out, so you should work on your character. Before you do anything for your pastor and before you serve him in any way, you must evaluate your character.

We will look at some critical character-building attitudes and behaviours that should be developed and discuss the significance and importance of these attributes for those who serve as Armorbearers.

A GOOD REPUTATION

Then the twelve summoned the multitude of the disciples and said, "It is not desirable that we should leave the word of God and serve tables. Therefore, brethren, seek out from among you seven men of good reputation, full of the Holy Spirit and wisdom, whom we may appoint over this business; but we will give ourselves continually to prayer and to the ministry of the word.

Acts 6:2-4

Notice that the persons who were to be chosen to serve tables had to be men of good reputation, full of the Holy Spirit and be wise, just to serve tables. The issue of character includes all of these attributes. It is important in Armorbearers because you are an extension of the one you serve. People will look at **you** and judge your pastor by **your** attitude and character.

When I first started working with Bishop Neil C. Ellis, I was not as polished as I am now (and there is still more polishing needed), but I remember wanting to go to certain places and wanting to do certain things, but the Holy Spirit reminded me who I was, and I remembered for whom I was working and that quickly caused me to change my direction. I realized because of this that there are certain places I cannot go, there are certain things that I cannot say, and there are certain things that I cannot do because of my assignment as an Armorbearer. People will look at me and come to conclusions about the one I serve. I have to be accountable for my actions because what I do and how I behave can have a significant affect on the ministry as a whole.

Work on your character. Try to be the best that you can be. Be honest in your dealings with others. If people have negative things to say about you, let it be a lie. You are not called to be perfect, but you should be the best you can be.

COMMITTED

Then Elijah said to him, "Elisha, stay here, please, for the LORD has sent me on to Jericho." But he said, "As the LORD lives, and as your soul lives, I will not leave you!" So they came to Jericho. Now the sons of the prophets who were at Jericho came to Elisha and said to him, "Do you know that the LORD will take away your master from over you today?" So he answered, "Yes, I know; keep silent!" Then Elijah said to him, "Stay here, please, for the LORD has sent me on to the Jordan." But he said, "As the LORD lives, and as your soul lives, I will not leave you!" So the two of them went on.

2 Kings 2:4-6

Armorbearers have to be committed to their pastors. This commitment is not only verbal, but it is demonstrated by your behavior and birthed out of your spirit. Those who bear arms for their leaders cannot quit in the middle of a battle. You have to defend and protect your pastor through every battle, and you have to stay until the end. That is the only way that you can protect.

Commitment to this assignment means that you will be **present**. Whenever your pastor serves and wherever your pastor serves, you should be present. Through every trial, every scandal, every lie, every attack of the enemy, your commitment to your pastor must remain steadfast. Commitment is when you make up your mind that no matter what happens you will remain faithful to the assignment. Staying is not always easy. If something goes wrong or something was not done, the Armorbearer is the first to receive rebuke. First of all, that is because you are present. Second of all, it is because your pastor has a certain expectation of you and that is that you would serve in such a way that there would be no problems. I know. Sometimes you do what you are supposed to do and still something goes wrong. It happens. Understand that you are being chastised and rebuked because you are present. Do not take offense to it. Make whatever remedy you can to the situation and then continue to serve.

Commitment includes serving in spite of opposition. Bishop Ellis always says that not everyone will like you. No matter how good you are, how spiritual you are or even how nice you are, there will be people close to you and in your ministry who will not like you. This is where you will be tested in your commitment to your assignment. When attacks are launched against you, your first thought is to leave. You say to yourself, "I don't have to take this," or "I don't need this aggravation" and you just want to resign—pack up your things and just leave. We have all been there. But here is the key—Armorbearers should support their pastors until the end. When this happens, you have to sharpen your focus toward your assignment. You have to look past the people, past the personalities, past your personal feelings and consider that your assignment requires you to serve your pastor with a committed heart. I want to encourage you to pray in these times of great opposition. That is not just a cliché. Simply go to God and tell him how you feel about what is happening to you, and ask him to help you to do what is necessary to fulfill your assignment. Ask Him to strengthen you so that you are not easily offended by the people who oppose you. Ask Him to give you the tenacity and the resilience to be in the presence of those who do not like you. God wants you to be successful in your service and if you ask Him, He will give you what you need to make it happen.

Commitment includes **sacrifice.** Armorbearers are always on duty even if they are not scheduled to serve in a particular service. Every time your pastor ministers, preaches, travels or serves in a gathering of people, those who bear arms (Armorbearers) should be ready to serve. Armorbearers must give time, effort, energy and financial resources in order to serve with excellence. When you take on the job of an Armorbearer, it simply means putting aside yourself as number one and focusing on the one to whom you have been assigned and to do it with a willing heart and without complaining. You must be committed to making your pastor's dream come alive even if it means putting your dream on hold. Don't underestimate this point. You have to be prepared to give all that you have so that your pastor's dream can come alive. This means serving despite your feelings, emotions and personal desires, which is the ultimate sacrifice.

GREAT PERCEPTION OF THE MAN OR WOMAN OF GOD

And she said unto her husband, Behold now, I perceive
that this is a holy man of God, which passeth by us
continually. Let us make a little chamber, I pray thee,
on the wall; and let us set for him there a bed, and a
table, and a stool, and a candlestick: and it shall be,
when he cometh to us that he shall turn in thither.
2 Kings 4:9-10 KJV

How you serve your pastor as an Armorbearer is directly related to how you **perceive** him. Be sure that you perceive your pastor as a holy man or woman of God before you accept the appointment to serve as an Armorbearer. This has to be settled in your heart and in your spirit because the quality of your service depends on it.

Whether you know it or not, people make careful observation of the way you serve and handle your pastor. They take cues from you as to how they will treat or revere your pastor. If you treat him with respect and honor, that is how others will treat him. If you are careless in the way you talk about him and do not honor him, then other people will treat your pastor with less respect than he deserves.

In every situation, you have to hold your pastor in high esteem. Even in light moments when you may be in an informal setting, be careful not to become too casual with your pastor. Even though my pastor, Bishop Neil C. Ellis, is my brother, I have always referred to him as Bishop. Even at family gatherings away from the church and away from ministry, I refer to him as Bishop. It is a matter of respect for the position he holds as God's voice in my life. The same should be true for you. No matter how close you think you are, do not let the **spirit of familiarity** cause you to lose the reverence for the man or woman of God you serve.

The respect that you have for your pastor should be so deep that even if he handles you in a manner that is painful, you can still see him as worthy of honor. Even with his limitations, inabilities, idiosyncrasies and other habits that you may or may not like, respect him for the office that he holds. He is the mouth-piece of God for your life. It's not about you and it's not really about him. It's about advancing the Kingdom and the power of God that will be shared with the people of God.

TRUSTWORTHY

I believe one of the most important characteristics in Armorbearers is that they are trustworthy. Your pastor should be able to trust you in many ways. Here are some of them:

Confidentiality: The Armorbearer spends a considerable amount of time with his leader and is privileged to see aspects of his character, personality and family that other people will never see. Armorbearers who serve their pastors have direct access to them, their conversations with members, telephone calls and other confidential information. With this privilege, you must be careful with the handling of information that you are privy to. It is not *public* information and it is not *your* information and so it should not be repeated or shared with anyone. Even if this information will be useful to defend your pastor, it should still not be shared. Developing this level of confidentiality may take time, but you have to keep it uppermost in your mind. Even the simplest details must be guarded.

Communication: As an Armorbearer, you are a target. There are some people who would like to know certain details about your pastor and about your ministry, and they view you as someone who could provide such insight. This makes you a target. Yes, you are a nice person, but everyone who befriends you does not have pure intentions. Be on guard that people may be using you to get information that they would not otherwise have access to. My advice to you is to learn how to perfect the art of silence.

Be soft-spoken and be slow to speak. Be quick to hear but slow to speak so that you do not get drawn into certain kinds of conversations. If you are naturally a good communicator, be especially careful. You might be well into sharing too much before you even realize it. Our own shortcomings can make us vulnerable. Keep in mind, though, that if you feel uncomfortable or that the information you are sharing is sensitive, you can do something about it. Just shift the conversation and talk about something else. Use those situations as a reminder for future situations.

Another aspect of communication involves communicating with your pastor. Your pastor has to know that you are sharing all information with him that should be communicated to him. For example, if people give you a message for your pastor, make sure that he gets it. If you cannot give it to him at that moment verbally, write it down and put it on his desk. When you speak with him again, be sure that he saw the message you left for him. Similarly, if he gives you a message for someone else, be sure that information is shared with the relevant parties.

Additionally, if you come into information that will help him in his assignment, let him know. Keep him informed about areas of ministry that you may have knowledge about that could affect him. If there are people who are creating difficulties for the ministry, share that information as well, at the appropriate time. Timing is everything. Observe your pastor so that you can determine when the best time is to talk to him, when not to talk to him and to understand the extent to which you can talk to him about various issues. When you understand these things, your communication with him will be at the best level.

Be a good listener. Sometimes all that is required as you communicate with your pastor is that you allow him a place to off-load some of the things that have weighed him down. This is where the element of trust becomes so important because in your act of listening, you are allowing ministry to happen for your pastor. This is a means of your supporting him, by allowing him to share this weight within the confines of confidentiality and privacy. Do not feel compelled to respond if your pastor is telling of his frustrations and demands of ministry. If you have to respond or feel compelled to do so, quote a scripture or assure him that you will make his concerns a matter of prayer.

Have his best interests at heart: Your pastor will trust you when he has seen that you have his best interest at heart. Notice that I used the past tense, when he has seen. That means that trust does not come right away. It has to be earned. You have to demonstrate that you are trustworthy by the way you handle yourself in various situations. Don't work for this, just serve with a pure heart and it will flow naturally. If you have pure intentions and serve with a good heart, your pastor will see that you have his best interests at heart.

Conclusion: The character of an Armorbearer must be developed. It does not come overnight, and it may not come easily, but there must be a concentrated effort to develop it. As your pastor's influence increases, your character must be upgraded to match because you are an extension. Your attitude and behaviour are always being observed by others, and you must operate with that in mind. You must be careful at all times not to bring shame to God, your pastor or the ministry by poor behavior on your part. If you fail in this area, your pastor's life, influence, impact and power in ministry could be hindered. You must succeed—and you can—work on it!

CHAPTER TWO

PREPARING YOURSELF FOR SERVICE

—ⵡ—

PERSONAL PREPARATION

"The preparations of the heart belong to man, but the answer of the tongue is from the LORD."

Proverbs 16:1

The road to preparation to serve your pastor began with a character check. Before you consider accepting this ministry assignment, you should be sure that you have passed the initial character test and still be prepared to work on it. The reason for that is because as you serve your pastor, new situations will arise that you will have to adapt to in order to carry out your assignment. If you believe that you have the right character for the job, it's time to prepare yourself to serve. This preparation is personal, emotional, mental, physical and spiritual. We will look at case studies of some Armorbearers in the Bible to reinforce the principles of this chapter.

Understanding the Pastor: The first step in supporting your pastor is getting to know him. You have to learn how he thinks, what he likes, what makes him angry, and what motivates him. As you learn what they like, those are the things you want to do and promote. The things that upset him and distract him from his ministry should be the things that you are careful to stay away from and also to prevent others from doing.

This mandate of getting to know the senior pastor should not encourage an Armorbearer to become overbearing or to constantly ask him questions. It is a type of knowing that is borne out of *observation and attention.* Pay attention to everything around you and observe your pastor's reactions and responses to people and events around him. As you do this, you will begin to see a pattern. This pattern should give you some insight as to what he likes and what he does not like. When you identify these traits, incorporate them into the way you serve. If your pastor doesn't like to talk much before they preach, then do not just stand there while many people try to talk to him before they preaches. Find a graceful way to interject and relieve him of that pressure. This is only one example, but the point is that you should take an active role to ensure that your pastor is in the best condition to execute his ministry assignment.

Understanding your pastor means that you have to get to know his heart and develop a spiritual connection. The heart of the pastor is normally articulated through his vision. It is the assignment for which God has anointed and gifted him. It is the vision that must be completed in the ministry and in a particular kind of way. The vision also details the pastor's plan or the method to be used in fulfilling this mandate.

Read your pastor's vision over and over so that you can understand him better and be able to give support where needed. As a matter of fact, one of the persons who should have the vision at heart should be the Armorbearer. If you are bearing arms, you must know what you are supporting. Not only should you know what you are supporting but you also should embody the vision. You should be the first example of what the pastor is trying to develop in the other members because you are closer to him than the others. If your pastor's vision calls for people to volunteer in the community, you should be a community volunteer. If prayer is a central focus in the vision, you should be a person of prayer. People should not be able to look at you and see you doing something that is diametrically opposed to the vision.

The Right Spirit: In order to be an effective aid to the pastor, an Armorbearer should have the pastor's spirit. To have the pastor's spirit is different from receiving the Holy Spirit. The Holy Spirit comes along as a help to you; you take on your pastor's spirit as a helper to him! God told Moses to gather the seventy elders who were his helpers,

> *"Then I will come down and talk with you there. I will take of the Spirit that is upon you and will put the same upon them; and they shall bear the burden of the people with you, that you may not bear it yourself alone."*
>
> **Numbers 11:17**

If you take on the spirit of the pastor, you will not follow your own agenda. When you take on the pastor's spirit, you will not talk about him in public nor will you allow others to speak disparagingly about him in your presence. You will not divulge things you have heard spoken in private to your neighbors and friends once you have finished serving. It may take some getting used to, but you have to be very careful about what you say about your pastor and your ministry even away from the church. Even in trying to defend your pastor, you could be unknowingly causing harm. The way to protect against this is not to discuss anything that you have heard while you were serving with anyone—including your family.

31

Personal preparation includes making a decision to live a holy life. This is what you do on a day-to-day basis "when no one is looking." Because you are a representative of the ministry and you want to protect its integrity, you should make a decision to live in such a way that God will be glorified through your behaviour.

Do not take your service for granted, and do not underestimate the value and importance of your assignment. Working closely with your pastor gives you the kind of access that others may want but do not have. The devil may try to attack you as a means of distracting the man or woman of God. In order to counteract any plan of the enemy, commit yourself and your service to God every time you have the opportunity to do so. It really should be a daily routine.

EMOTIONAL PREPARATION

The Armorbearer must be emotionally prepared when serving the pastor. Your service and your support of the pastor should not be contingent upon your feelings and your emotions. You must serve well when you feel like it, when you do not feel like it, when all is well in your personal life and when things may not be well. While you may be experiencing difficult situations in your personal life, you must not allow this to distract you from your service.

You must serve well when the pastor praises you as well as the times when you are rebuked. If you are rebuked, do not take on the *spirit of offense*. This is where you "harbor" bad feelings because of that chastening or rebuke. I know it is hard but you should receive the chastisement and use it to help you serve better. As an Armorbearer especially, there are times when you feel neglected and overlooked because your service is transparent, but you have to keep a good spirit. Emotional preparation will help you to do this. No chastening seems good for the moment but it helps us to bear fruit. Your pastor wants what is best for you despite how you feel about what he does. Keep it all in perspective and do not allow your emotions to get the best of you.

You must also be mentally prepared for the names the people will call you and the challenges you will face just because of your position. Not everyone will like you and not everyone is happy about your presence. People will call you names and they will make you the subject of many rumors and lies because they envy the position you hold. I will admit, sometimes it can get very difficult, but I want to encourage you to toughen up your emotions and keep serving. Don't allow the liars and the agents of the enemy to kill your spirit or move you out of your divine assignment. Take it in stride and stay focused on your assignment. God will not let them have the last say.

Armorbearers are people too, they have feelings, desires and needs like other members of the congregation, but they are chosen to carry out a very important task—to serve the man or woman of God. This position is not to be taken lightly. The overall object of the Armorbearer's service is to ensure that the vision of the pastor is fulfilled and that he is able to impart, with minimum hindrance, the word of God to the people of God. You must be settled in your mind and spirit early that you have been chosen for a job that many others may want but are not anointed for. Thank God you have been anointed, for it and you had better make sure that you are prepared.

PHYSICAL PREPARATION

Physical preparation for an Armorbearer is important for several reasons.

Good Health: The first reason to prepare physically is for good health. This means eating properly so that your body has its entire requirement for proper functioning. An Armorbearer who is sick regularly cannot help effectively.

Energy: It takes a lot of energy to keep up with your pastor. If you look at the job of an Armorbearer from the outside, you will believe it is an easy task, but trust me, if your pastor is anything like Bishop Neil C. Ellis of Nassau, Bahamas, you will need your vitamins and you will need to stay in shape. If you travel with your pastor, you need to do what you must to ensure that you are able to support fully. This means that you should not be tired, slothful or sleepy while you are serving. A tired Armorbearer is a dangerous person. You need energy so that you can be alert, focused and attentive in your assignment and to increase your fortitude and patience for the long hours of service.

Armorbearers should be physically fit to be able to endure the spiritual and emotional demands they will encounter while serving their pastors. You should secure the best workout schedule to ensure regular exercise to build enough fortitude and energy to keep up with your pastor. There is such a heavy mandate on some of our pastors that it makes it hard for them to slow down, so you need to pick it up.

Vitamins, food supplements, exercise, energy bars and a well-balanced diet are all aspects of physical preparation that will be important factors in **how** you serve.

Deportment: Physical preparation also includes how you look—your deportment. As an extension of the pastor, an Armorbearer should always be properly attired. Your clothing should be clean, pressed and suitable for the occasion. Females should take care to ensure that their clothing is not revealing or close-fitting. Footwear should be cleaned or polished, suitable and comfortable as long periods of standing may be required. Your face should be clean, shaven and properly prepared. Makeup for women should me moderately applied and not too heavy. Again, you do not want to attract attention to yourself while you are serving.

Hairstyles should be moderate and not too overwhelming for the same reason.

Hygiene is also an important element of deportment. A fresh breath and pleasant smelling body odor is mandatory for the Armorbearer. Take extra care to ensure that if people smell you that it is a pleasant aroma that they encounter. You should carry with you the items that are necessary to keep this area under control. Female Armorbearers must compensate for the changes in the body that occur during their menstrual cycle and properly prepare to handle this situation.

Good health, energy, exercise and deportment are important aspects. The best preparation you can make to help your pastor is to make sure that you are prepared. If you are prepared well, then you are in a better position to support your pastor.

MENTAL PREPARATION

As an Armorbearer, you have to be mentally prepared to serve. Mental preparation means that your mind is fully engaged in fulfilling your assignment. It means that you are not distracted by some thought or activity that is not presently related to your service. As you serve, you must be single-minded in the purpose for which you have been called. This section discusses how you can achieve these goals.

Stay focused: Keeping the right focus means that you keep an optimistic outlook. No matter the failures of the day, you look with bright hope to tomorrow and what you will be able to accomplish. Keeping the right focus implies that:

- You understand your individual assignment.
- You do not pay attention to negative comments about your assignment.
- You are sure about the call of God on your life.

- You are not distracted by what others are doing or how they have been gifted.
- You kill the spirit of jealousy.
- You will not allow others to throw you off course.

The right focus forces you to concentrate on the power of God working in you and not in your own ability. The right focus points to God and recognizes that you are only His agent.

Don't take it personally: There are times when it may seem like the pastor is harsh in giving commands, but the Armorbearer must not take this personally. If you are mentally prepared, you would recognize or discern the forces operating inside and around the pastor that may have made his command seem harsh. Also, with the correct mental preparation, the Armorbearer would not accept the command as harsh. The testimony of David's reaction to King Saul when he continuously chased him trying to kill him is an excellent example of not taking it personally. David did not try to kill Saul even when he had the opportunity. David understood his place, and Armorbearers must know theirs. You must recognize that God has chosen you to minister to His anointed and personal feelings have to be set aside.

Rejuvenate yourself: Don't allow yourself to become "overwhelmed." Low mental energy leaves you open to attack on the mind from the enemy and may lead to feelings of envy, jealousy, insecurity, unworthiness, incompetence and insufficiency. If you find yourself in this state, look for some additional support and take a break so that you can rejuvenate yourself.

You can experience success as an Armorbearer or experience total failure as a result of your mental preparedness or lack thereof. If you lose the battle in your mind, as to what you are called to do and how you should be doing it, then you have lost victory in your assignment. If you win the battle in your mind, then you will have victory in your assignment as well.

SPIRITUAL PREPARATION

The church has too many carnal people serving in high positions. We do not need any more un-spiritual Armorbearers in the Kingdom of God. There must be spiritual maturity in the life of the Armorbearer, and that comes through Bible study, prayer, intercession and fasting. You should be so prepared spiritually that you can discern what is going on and intercede, thus making the burden lighter for your pastor.

Bible study: Spiritually, an Armorbearer should have a lifestyle of prayer and studying of God's Word. Prayer meeting and Bible study must be on your list of services to attend on a weekly basis. Continual prayer and reading of God's Word will also empower the Armorbearer to deal with forces in his own life. As you know more of the Word of God, then the enemy will have less power to deceive you or to distract you from your ministry. The Bible says that "people perish for the lack of knowledge." This means then that we succeed once we have knowledge. Your study of the Bible should cause you to not only have knowledge but also wisdom as to the things you should do and those you should refrain from as you serve the man or woman of God.

Prayer: We mentioned earlier that Armorbearers should pray for themselves; to keep themselves girded against the attack of the enemy. But you cannot stop there. Because of the unique access you have to the man or woman of God, you are aware of other issues that may hinder the ministry as a whole. In your private time, you should put these matters in prayer before God.

You should also be sure to attend corporate prayer meetings so that you can maintain your connection to the ministry. Even while you are in service, there will be many forces attempting to hinder the message your pastor has to deliver. An Armorbearer is also driven to prayer if the message being preached seems to be a hard one to deliver, asking God to help the pastor to deliver the sermon with strength and clarity and also that the people will be receptive to the Word.

Intercession: Praying regularly for your pastor and the ministry as a whole is literally the best gift you can give your pastor. It will not only be incredibly supportive and encouraging, but will also produce dramatic effects. If you are aware of specific needs in the life of the pastor, you should present those needs before the Lord in prayer. You should pray for your pastor daily with special emphasis on his family, his vision, his relationship with God and the congregation.

Fasting: An Armorbearer should regularly fast for the ministry and the assignment they have been given. Fasting is the Armorbearer"s way of asking God to intervene and rule over his service. It is his way of admitting that in and of himself, they are not able to complete this work on his own and invoking God's help and direction. My Pastor, Bishop Neil C. Ellis, whom I have served for the past ten years, wrote a book entitled, *Fasting for Results.* In it he talks about nine kinds of fasts in the Bible that are briefly outlined here:

1. **The Disciples Fast** – The purpose of this fast is "to loose the bands of wickedness" and free ourselves and others from addictions to sins.
2. **The Ezra Fast** – The purpose of this fast is to "undo heavy burdens" – to solve problems, to invite the Holy Spirit's aid in lifting loads and overcoming barriers that keep you and your loved ones from living a victorious life.
3. **The Samuel Fast** – The purpose of this fast is to "let the oppressed (physically and spiritually) go free." This fast is for the oppressed who need to be free and the spiritual leaders who will minister to them.

4. **The Elijah Fast** – The purpose of this fast is to "break every yoke" in an effort to conquer the mental and emotional problems that would control our lives. This fast is designed to help break negative mental and emotional habits.

5. **The Widow's Fast** – The purpose of this fast is to care for the poor and needy and meet the humanitarian needs of others. This fast is for those who choose to sacrifice their own needs to meet the critical needs of others.

6. **The Saint Paul's Fast** – The purpose of this fast is to seek God's help in bringing about a clearer perspective and insight as you make crucial decisions. This fast is for those who need insight and wisdom from God in their decision making.

7. **The Daniel Fast** – This fast is designed to bring you physical health and healing, spiritual wisdom and insight or a spiritual breakthrough.

8. **The John the Baptist Fast** – The purpose of this fast is "that your righteousness shall go before you," that your testimony and influence for Christ will be enhanced before others. This fast is designed to expand your testimony and increase your influence for God.

9. **The Esther Fast** – The purpose of this fast is that "the glory of the Lord" will protect us from the evil one. This fast is intended to protect you from evil for the glory of God.

Adapted from "Fasting for Results Study Guide" by Bishop Neil C. Ellis Legacy Publishers International 2006

I cannot stress enough that the armorbearer must be spiritual. After all, you are an aide to God's mouthpiece, and being spiritual can only serve to help you to become a successful armorbearer.

APPLICATION OF YOUR PREPARATION

The personal, emotional, physical, mental and spiritual preparation of the Armorbearer which we have previously discussed is all toward the end of lifting, supporting and serving the senior pastor. I want to talk about two of the main applications of your preparation to serve.

MAKE HIM LOOK GOOD

Everything you do as an Armorbearer will reflect on your pastor whether for good or for evil. You have to purpose in your psyche to do the things that will make your pastor look good and to be highly regarded by others.

You make your pastor look good when you serve with excellence. When you display proficiency in your assignment, you make your pastor look good. When you think about five-star restaurants and five-star hotels, the only difference between them and other hotels and restaurants with lower ratings is the level of service given by the staff. It cannot be a five-star hotel with two-star service, when the maid does not come to clean the room everyday and there is no bell service and no concierge. In other words, your pastor will not be highly regarded if you display a bad attitude and disrespect others around you. The pastor will be five-star when you serve in a manner that is of high quality.

You make him look good by having a pleasant attitude and getting along with others. It can be very stressful to a pastor to have those who serve close to him in constant conflict with others. Not only is it a poor reflection but it also creates tension and distraction. Avoid petty arguments and behavior among those who serve with you. Don't hold on to offenses and try to keep a good working environment around the pastor.

You make your pastor look good when you make things happen. Take some initiative to do some things on behalf of your pastor for the people who are close to him. Honor his or her spouse by serving him or her when you have opportunity. Remind your pastor about engagements and assignments that may be forgotten and make sure that they do not forget important dates (birthdays, anniversaries, etc).

There are many other ways in which you can make your pastor look good. We cannot cover them all here, but the spirit is what is most important. If you know of things to do that will cause the pastor to be highly regarded in the ministry and in the community, then you should endeavor to do those things.

COVER YOUR PASTOR

"Covering" your pastor is an expression that suggests that an Armorbearer must be in position. You should not be caught off guard or out of position where you cannot protect your pastor. Here are some ways to "cover your pastor."

In Luke 8, we read of the woman with the issue of blood who touched the hem of Jesus' garment and was healed. I want to draw your attention to some other elements of the story. When Jesus asked the disciples who touched Him, they were amazed at Jesus' question because there were so many people around him. Here is what Jesus said in response, "I felt virtue leave me." Now here was a woman who, according to law, should not even be out in public. Similarly, there are people in your church who have ulterior motives for being there. As an Armorbearer you have to cover and protect your pastor because if virtue left Jesus and a pastor is vulnerable after preaching, if somebody gets to him who should not get to him, that person can bring harm. You have to protect.

You cover your pastor by keeping private things private. There are some broken things in the life of your pastor—every one has them—but you have to keep the cover closed while the Lord helps him to fix them. If for some reason he has shared them with you or allowed you to see them, it is because he trusts you. He trusts you to cover him in prayer through encouragement and support and in keeping his private matters private.

One definition of the word "cover" is to "be enough money to take care of." There are times while you are working with your pastor that you will have to pay for some things out of your own pocket. You have to be prepared to do this and consider it as a seed into his life. For example, when your pastor is traveling, he is so focused in where he is headed that he often overlooks the skycap, the bellman and other services that require tipping. If you received a per diem to pay for these items, use it. If you did not receive a per diem, you should cover these expenses from your resources to make sure that your pastor does not appear mean simply because his focus is elsewhere at the time.

While you are working and covering your pastor, you are learning. You are being trained and developed. You are getting some skills which will be imparted to you that you may not receive through formal education. That impartation you will only receive if you stay close and cover your pastor.

CHAPTER THREE

PREPARING TO SERVE
WITHIN SET BOUNDARIES

—ᴍ—

In the last chapter, we talked about how Armorbearers prepare themselves to serve. However, Armorbearers do not serve in a vacuum, so we have to understand that personal preparation in the wider context of ministry. Because an Armorbearer has prepared himself or herself to serve does not mean that he or she will serve in an excellent manner. It is possible to prepare well and still encounter failure in the assignment. In this chapter, we will look at **three** important areas that must be attended to properly if an Armorbearer is to be successful in his or her assignment. Pay close attention, because your ministry will be greatly affected by how well you can implement these principles. The chapter closes with case studies of some Armorbearers and what you can learn from their service to make your service more effective.

UNDERSTANDING THE ENVIRONMENT

Being an Armorbearer means working closely with your pastor. This means that you may have the opportunity of knowing him both publicly and privately. The Armorbearer is one of the persons outside of the pastor's immediate family who is closest to him. He is privy to the good days and the not so good days of the pastor. Despite this fact, you must recognize that **your pastor has a private life and a private sphere of operation that does not necessarily include you.** You should respect his private and personal space.

You should not pry into the pastor's personal life or engage in any personal discussions without his invitation. Too often Armorbearers become too comfortable around their pastors and allow a spirit of familiarity to set in. You should guard yourself against this temptation. You and your pastor are not on the same level. No matter how close you become as you serve, you must always keep your pastor in high esteem and be careful not to overstep the boundary of a "helper."

As an Armorbearer, if you have knowledge of the private affairs of the pastor, then they are to remain "private." You should never discuss those matters with anyone at any time, not even to defend the pastor. A lot of times, Armorbearers cause harm in these issues while trying to do good. Let private matters be private matters and respect the privacy and personal space of the one you serve.

When your pastor is engaged in conversation, you should take a step back. You are not a part of the conversation and you should not be involved in it. If you are serving during this time, then you should stand quietly, scanning the surrounding area in case there is unsuspecting danger.

DEFINING THE BOUNDARIES

You have not been chosen as an Armorbearer to be a broker or an agent for your personal gain. In other words, you should not use your connection to your pastor as some sort of bargaining tool or some birthright to be sold for your benefit. As you begin to serve your pastor, you will gain some recognition from others as being close to him. Some persons who would like to have access to your pastor for one reason or another might view you as someone who can open a door for them. Don't allow yourself to become involved in these situations—they have the potential to create divided loyalties. Your focus should always be on your assignment because a divided focus is a detriment.

As an Armorbearer, you only have as much authority as your pastor gives you. Do not take it upon yourself to speak for your pastor or on behalf of your pastor when he has not given you the permission to do so. People may believe you because they know of your connection to the pastor, but let me tell you, God sees all and knows all and He pays us according to our works. Later in this chapter, we will see what Gehazi got for this kind of behavior. Let me hasten to tell you that it was death. In today's environment, death does not have to be only physical. It can be a loss of influence, loss of integrity and even worse, loss of connection with God and your God-ordained connection, your pastor.

Similarly, as Armorbearers, you must be careful NOT TO overstep your boundaries. If you have been given an assignment and you do not complete it, that is disobedience, and disobedience should not be an acceptable behavioural trait in Armorbearers.

RESPECTING THE PASTOR'S FAMILY

This is, in my opinion, one of the most important areas that must be respected and highly regarded by Armorbearers who serve in the Church today. Many Armorbearers have failed in their assignment because they did not show sufficient regard for the pastor's family. You do not have to fail in this manner, and succeeding is not as difficult as you think.

Respect for your pastor's spouse

You should respect your pastor's spouse in the same way that you respect your pastor. Whatever you would do for your pastor as you serve him should be done the same manner that you should offer for the spouse. If you open the door for your pastor and you have opportunity, you should do the same for his spouse. You cannot demonstrate that you care for and respect your pastor if you cannot demonstrate that same care and concern for the spouse and by extension, his children. You should take extra care to look out for and bless the family of the pastor you serve, especially if the pastor is not present.

The pastor's family should receive all of the graces that are due to them. You cannot honor the pastor and dishonor his family. You cannot respect the pastor and disrespect his family. Armorbearers should look out for the pastor's entire family.

Respect for the Marriage Bond

Your Pastor's marriage, like every other marriage, is a sacred bond and it must be respected. If you are serving your pastor and his spouse comes into your midst, you should give your regards and excuse yourself unless otherwise advised. By doing this, you are saying by your actions that you respect the marriage bond. At the appropriate time, if necessary, your pastor may ask you to re-enter. This is the case if he meets in person or if it is a phone call. No matter what the medium, it is your action of respecting the pastor's position that is important.

Developing Relationship

In order to care for the pastor's family, you have to know them. If you don't know them personally, then you at least need to know what his expectations are of you. What does your pastor expect of you as it relates to dealing with his family? What does the spouse expect from you? If you don't know, then you should pause and ask him.

As you interact with your pastor, you should be cognizant of your own behaviour. Do not infringe on his private time with his family. Do not invade his personal space. As you serve with sensitivity toward the family of the pastor, you will develop the kind of relationship that will make your service successful.

An Armorbearer's role is one of interesting dichotomies and defined boundaries. You should be close enough to serve the pastor but distant enough to respect his personal space. You should be in close proximity in order to protect him but inconspicuous enough so that you are not a distraction as you serve. You must know enough about the pastor to serve him effectively, but that information must not be exposed to outside parties. Is it all just a bunch of rules to be followed? I don't think so. Armorbearers are much more important than that. As we review the case studies below, we will see the importance of their service.

BIBLICAL CASE STUDIES

For the purposes of these case studies, let us review the definition of an Armorbearer. An Armorbearer is a person who walks with, holds up and protects the senior pastor and does what is necessary to help him fulfill and bring to pass his God-given vision. It is important to keep this definition in mind as we look at the actions of some Armorbearers in Scripture. I am not suggesting that these Armorbearers were successes or failures; I am simply highlighting specific behaviours which will provide some important information to help you in your assignment.

AARON AND HUR

And so it was, when Moses held up his hand, that Israel prevailed; and when he let down his hand, Amalek prevailed. But Moses' hands became heavy; so they took a stone and put it under him and he sat on it. And Aaron and Hur supported his hands, one on one side and the other on the other side and his hands were steady until the going down of the sun. So Joshua defeated Amalek and his people with the edge of the sword.

Exodus 17:11-13

Aaron and Hur saw a need that Moses had and sought to fulfill it. The Scripture does not indicate that Moses called for them to help him. When they saw that Moses' hands became heavy, they put a stone under him so that he could rest. They came to Moses because they wanted to help him. As they came to meet the first need they saw, they realized another need and then sought to meet that need also by holding up his hand. That is what Armorbearers do. They come to meet a need and they stay until the assignment is completed.

RUTH AND NAOMI

"And she said, "Look, your sister-in-law has gone back to her people and to her gods; return after your sister-in-law. But Ruth said,
"Entreat me not to leave you,
Or to turn back from following after you;
For wherever you go, I will go;
And wherever you lodge, I will lodge;
Your people shall be my people,
And your God, my God,
Where you die,

I will die and there will I be buried.
The LORD do so to me and more also,
lif anything but death parts you and me."
Ruth 1:15-17 (emphasis added)

Naomi entreated her daughters-in-law Ruth and Orpah to depart from her after the death of their husbands who were her sons. She gave them an opportunity to leave. Ruth refused. In fact, she not only refused to leave Naomi, she made a commitment to serve her until death parts them.

Because of her connection to Naomi's family, Ruth followed Naomi into territory that was unfamiliar to her. In following Naomi, Ruth did not know where she was going or where she would end up, but she was sure of one thing—wherever Naomi went, she would go with her. She was steadfast in her commitment to be with Naomi. When they got to Bethlehem, Ruth gathered grain for them to eat. Ruth did what her mother-in-law asked her to do, and she was obedient to the commands of Naomi. What is clear in the story of Ruth and Naomi is that Ruth submitted herself to her mother-in-law and was careful to heed the advice she got from her. Ruth was open to the advice of Naomi. She did not second-guess her and she did not disobey her. Scripture bears this out in Ruth 3:5 when Ruth says to Naomi, "All that you say, to me I will do." This was characteristic of their relationship.

Ruth's commitment to Naomi caused Naomi to be well regarded in her community, according to Ruth 4:15, "And may he be a restorer of life and a nourisher of your old age; for your daughter-in-law, who loves you, who is better to you than seven sons, has borne him." Ruth's service to Naomi was not motivated by selfishness. She cared for Naomi and served and cared for her because of the respect she had for her. As a result of their relationship, Ruth's life was blessed and Naomi's life was blessed as well.

JONATHAN AND HIS ARMORBEARER

Then Jonathan said to the young man who bore his armor, "Come let us go over to the garrison of these uncircumcised; it may be that the LORD will work for us. For nothing restrains the LORD from saving by many or by few. So his armorbearer said to him, "Do all that is in your heart. Go then; here I am with you, according to your heart. Then Jonathan said, "Very well, let us cross over to these men and we will show ourselves to them.

1 Samuel 14:6-8

Jonathan's armorbearer was more than just an aide or servant; he was a loyal partner in battle. Jonathan's armorbearer says to him, "Do all that is in your heart. Go then, I am here with you according to your heart." This response is given as two Israelites (Jonathan and his armorbearer) attempt to fight an entire army of Philistines. The armorbearer didn't say, "We should not pursue this army;" he did not say, "Let's get the other Israelites to go with us;" and he did not say, "They are too many for us, they will kill us." He did what armorbearers should do, which is to encourage and to stand with their leaders once they have taken a position. In essence, Jonathan declared, "We can win; God can save by many or by few." The armorbearer's response shows that he had confidence in his leader and in effect says, "If you see victory, let us pursue it and even if we are not victorious, I will be faithful to bear arms for you until death." Your pastor deserves an armorbearer like that.

ELIJAH AND ELISHA

*Then Elijah said to him, "Elisha, stay here, please,
for the LORD has sent me on to Jericho." But he
said, "As the LORD lives, and as your soul lives, I
will not leave you!" So they came to Jericho. Now
the sons of the prophets who were at Jericho came to
Elisha and said to him, "Do you know that the LORD
will take away your master from over you today?"
So he answered, "Yes, I know; keep silent!" Then
Elijah said to him, "Stay here, please, for the LORD
has sent me on to the Jordan." But he said, "As the
LORD lives, and as your soul lives, I will not leave
you!" So the two of them went on.*

2 Kings 2:4-6

The obvious characteristic in this scripture is that
Armorbearers stick it out. They stay, they serve and they
support. Even when his leader gives Elisha the option to
leave, he refuses. He knew that his assignment was not
complete and so he stayed. Armorbearers who succeed have
this same determination to serve their leaders. Leaving is not
an option even if it is extended. Faithful armorbearers make
up their minds from the beginning of their appointments that
they will serve until the end of the assignment.

In this scripture, however, I want to draw attention to
another important character trait in Armorbearers and that is
that they do not allow others to pull them away from their
assignments. In verse five, the sons of the prophets attempt to
break Elisha's spirit by telling him that his leader was about
to die. In other words, they wanted him to leave his assignment because of what seemed to be impending doom. His
words to them were swift: "Yes, I know; keep silent." He did
not allow them to continue to speak negatively concerning
his leader. This is what you must do also. Do not allow others

to talk disparagingly about your leader. It does not matter if what they are saying is true or not. The bottom line is that they should not be comfortable with that kind of conversation around you. The language you have concerning your pastor should be a language of honor, esteem and respect. You should demand that of others around you as well. When they speak about your leader it should not be in a negative tone. Once people conclude that you will not accept defamatory conversations about your pastor, they will not do so in your presence.

ABIMELECH AND HIS ARMORBEARER

The he called quickly to the young man, his armorbearer, and said to him, "Draw your sword and kill me, lest men say of me, "A woman killed him." So his young man thrust him through, and he died.

Judges 9:54

Some people may look at this passage and conclude that Abimelech's armorbearer was faithful in that he obeyed Abimelech's command or that he preserved the dignity of his leader. What I would like to say here is that an Armorbearer should be careful not to "touch God's anointed"—the one whom they have been commanded to protect. Compare this armorbearer to Saul's armorbearer in 1 Samuel 31:4 who was asked to do the same thing;

Then Saul said to his armorbearer, "Draw your sword, and thrust me through with it, lest these uncircumcised men come and thrust me through and abuse me." But his armorbearer would not, for he was greatly afraid. Therefore Saul took a sword and fell on it. And when his armorbearer saw that

Saul was dead, he also fell on his sword, and died with him."

1 Samuel 31:4-5

In the same position, Saul's armorbearer refused to kill him. He was very careful not to touch his leader.

JOAB AND DAVID

Now the king had commanded Joab, Abishai and Ittai saying, "Deal gently for my sake with the young man Absalom. And all the people heard when the king gave all the captains orders concerning Absalom . . . .Now a certain man saw it and told Joab, and said, "I just saw Absalom hanging in a terebinth tree." So Joab said to the man who told him, ". . . .And why did you not strike him there to the ground? I would have given you ten shekels of silver and a belt." But the man said to Joab, "Though I were to receive a thousand shekels of silver in my hand, I would not raise my hand against the king's son. For in our hearing the king commanded you and Abishai and Ittai, saying, "Beware lest anyone touch the young man Absalom . . . . Then Joab said, "I cannot linger with you. And he took three spears in his hand and thrust them through Absalom's heart, while he was still alive in the midst of the terebinth tree.

2 Samuel 18: 5, 10-12, 14

Joab was David's commander in chief. He was a loyal supporter of David and he was a great warrior. He was revered by the men who submitted to his leadership. However, amidst his skill and commitment to David there are some points of interest for the Armorbearer.

First of all, David gave a specific command for Joab and the other leaders not to harm Absalom. This command was not given in private but in the public such that many others heard him say it. When the man told Joab that he saw Absalom, Joab's first response was that this man should have killed him and that he would have rewarded him for so doing. This is in direct opposition to David's command. Joab's response shows that his anger for Absalom was stronger than his commitment to his leader.

Secondly, Joab continues to pursue Absalom even after the man reminds him that the king gave specific instructions not to touch Absalom. The man again tells of the fact that many people were present when the king gave the decree. Nevertheless, Joab is not restrained.

Finally, he kills Absalom. Absalom was the king's son. We talked earlier about the fact that an Armorbearer should care for the pastor's family, not just the pastor alone. Someone could make the case that Absalom deserved to die and maybe even that Joab was defending the kingship of David through his actions. In a book of another title, that might be an argument to pursue. However, in this work where the focus is singularly on the attitude and service of Armorbearers, Joab must be considered for his disobedience to the direct command of his leader and for killing a member of his king's family. In fact, I would venture to say that Joab was more concerned with preserving his reputation as a ruthless warrior than he was in serving the king. This can never be accepted as a successful end for an Armorbearer.

NOAH AND HAM:

And Noah began to be a farmer, and he planted a vineyard. Then he drank of the wine and was drunk, and became uncovered in his tent. And Ham, the

father of Canaan, saw the nakedness of his father,
and told his two brothers outside.

Genesis 9:20-22

When Ham saw that his father was "uncovered," he went outside and told his brothers. On the face of this scripture, there may not seem to be anything wrong with Ham's going to tell his brothers about what he had seen, but if we follow the principle, he has failed in his call to support his father.

But Shem and Japheth took a garment, laid it both
on their shoulders, and went backward and covered
the nakedness of their father. Their faces were turned
away, and they did not see their father's nakedness.

Genesis 9:23

The other brothers' reaction to the same problem was totally different. Their leader, who was also their father, was in a condition that would bring shame to him, and so they did what was necessary to protect his reputation. Ham made no attempt to help his father. His first response was to go out and tell others about what he had seen in the private quarters of his father.

Our leaders are human and they may make mistakes that may cause embarrassment. As an Armorbearer, you should not seek to expose that information but instead you should do all you can to "cover your pastor," not cover up but cover. Further, when you see the aspects of your pastor's character that are not flattering, it should drive you to prayer not to gossip. When Noah recovered, he cursed Ham and all of his descendants. That is the reward for someone who is given the responsibility to cover his leader but instead chooses to expose him. Don't let that be your inheritance!

ELISHA AND GEHAZI:

But Gehazi, the servant of Elisha the man of God, said, "Look, my master has spared Naaman this Syrian, while not receiving from his hands what he brought, but as the LORD lives, I will run after him and take something from him. So Gehazi pursued Naaman. When Naaman saw him running after him, he got down from the chariot to meet him and said, "Is all well?" And he said, "All is well. My master has sent me, saying, indeed just now two young men of the sons of the prophets have come to me from the mountains of Ephraim. Please give them a talent of silver and two changes of garments . . . .Now he went in and stood before his master. Elisha said to him, "Where did you go, Gehazi?" And he said, "Your servant did not go anywhere."

2 Kings 5:20-22, 25

Do you see the problem? I know you do. Gehazi's first problem was that he thought that he knew better than his leader. He was probably upset that Elisha did not accept the gifts offered by Naaman. He disagreed with his leader and this disagreement cause him to take matters into his own hand. The second problem, birthed from the first problem, is that Gehazi operated outside of the boundaries of his authority. He told Naaman that Elisha had sent him and that was not true. Elisha did not send Gehazi to Naaman nor did he approve of Gehazi's actions. Gehazi's final and fatal error was then to lie to Elisha about what he had done. He undermined his leader, he misrepresented his leader, and then he lied to try to cover it all up. Whatever Gehazi's motives, his actions are indicative of an Armorbearer that should not maintain such a position with his leader.

You should not second-guess your leader. You are there to help not to lead. You do not have all of the facts, and what may seem to you to be a good decision has the potential to bring harm. You should not speak for your pastor unless you have been authorized to do so. This is an abuse of your association and service. Finally, NEVER lie to your leader. Your leader should be able to trust you. If you cannot be trusted to tell the truth, you cannot be trusted to serve.

ARE YOU READY?

Whew! That's a lot. Do you feel like this is too much for you? You didn't know all of this was required? You don't even know IF you CAN do all of these things? Don't lose heart and don't quit. If God, through your pastor, has assigned you to this role, God will empower you to fulfill it just as he did with Solomon in 1 Chronicles 28:10, ". . . for the LORD has chosen you to build a house for the sanctuary; be strong and do it." God makes provision for the assignment He has given you. If you have been chosen to serve in this role, you should feel privileged because it is a job of honor, but more importantly it says something about you. Let me tell you what it says:

1. Your pastor sees potential in you.
2. Your pastor trusts you.
3. Your pastor believes in you.
4. Your life has been shaped to enable you to fulfill this assignment.
5. You are able to be successful if you stay focused.

Now that you are prepared to serve, let's look at the practical aspects of serving your pastor as an Armorbearer.

CHAPTER FOUR

PREPARING FOR THE SENIOR PASTOR

—m—

There are many ways to serve the senior pastor. We will explore these areas where the armorbearer is expected to perform on a regular basis. These responsibilities will be presented in the form of practical steps to allow for easy understanding and implementation.

A. PREPARING FOR THE ARRIVAL OF THE PASTOR

Prior to arriving at church on a Sunday morning, the Armorbearer should be aware of the items needed for use that day so that they can be available for use. These items may include drinks, lozenges, etc. It may also be helpful to check with the church administrator to see if any guests are scheduled to be in attendance so that preparation can be made for them as well.

Arrive at least 45 minutes before pastor is expected to arrive: Armorbearers should be at the church (or location of engagement) at least 45 minutes before the start of a regular

Sunday service and at least an hour for special services and conferences. This lead time is for the Armorbearer to become settled and mentally prepared to serve. If you are rushing around to complete tasks just before the beginning of the service, you are bound to forget something,, misplace something or frustrate your pastor because of your lack of preparation. To avoid this, you should be prompt so that you can become familiar about the events of the day and the order of the service so that you are properly prepared to serve. On arrival the Armorbearer should check with the church administrator or executive pastor for any special information about the service that the pastor should be aware of. The Armorbearer should also be aware of this information to ensure that everything needed for the day is prepared and in place.

There should be at least two Armorbearers on duty to receive the senior pastor. One Armorbearer can prepare the items required for service (interior) and the other to await the arrival of the pastor (exterior). The exterior Armorbearer waits on the outside of the pastor's office in order to properly receive him and his family.

B. RECEIVING THE SENIOR PASTOR

Make sure the office is opened: If you do not have keys for the pastor's office, make sure that the executive assistant opens it in enough time to prepare for the pastor's arrival.

Prepare the office: The Armorbearer must prepare the office for the pastor's arrival. Always have bottled water available and prepare tea or coffee according to his preference. Know the brand he likes and the manner in which he likes it prepared (with or without cream, sugar or honey etc.). If breakfast and or fruits are the norm for the pastor, arrange him appropriately. Check the bathrooms to ensure they are clean, smelling fresh and have all of the necessary items the pastor may need. Ensure the air conditioning is on at a comfortable level and any other personal requests of the pastor are honored.

Receiving the Pastor: Ensure that the pastor's parking space is kept clear as you await his arrival. If there are parishioners who need to drop off items for the pastor or make attempts to meet with him, this Armorbearer can act as a receiver.

You should not become distracted by other activities around you so that you miss your pastor when he arrives. You should be alert with your hands free and ready to open the door.

When the pastor arrives, the car doors are opened by the Armorbearers as a matter of courtesy. When you do this, allow him to speak first, listen to all that he has to say to ensure you receive directives or questions. Receive whatever he has in his hands. Do not ask if you can take it; just say: "Bishop/ Pastor, let me take that for you." Keep his hands clear for anything that they may need to do or for people they may want to greet on his way to the office. What further action you take is dependant on what the pastor has requested of you. If there are no directives then the Armorbearer leads the pastor and his or her family to the office, opening all of the intermittent doors and ensuring that they are not interrupted or distracted along the way. If you are serving in inclement weather, be sure to have the necessary items handy to protect your pastor, including umbrella, flashlight or other protective instruments.

C. <u>PREPARING THE PASTOR'S GARMENTS FOR SERVICE</u>

Preparing the Garments: The Interior Armorbearer is also responsible for the pastor's garments. They should be inspected to ensure that they are clean, lint-free and pressed.

Any loose threads or missing buttons should be mended or an alternate garment should be used. The pastor's garments should be prepared and ready to be worn on his arrival if the garments are kept at the church. The bottom line here is that when the pastor mounts the pulpit in his clothes or official garments, they should be immaculate and without blemish. More information about the garments is covered later in the chapter.

Before the pastor leaves the office for the pulpit, make a quick check to ensure that all of his garments or clothes are prepared and that his shoes are clean.

Caring for the Garments: Your pastor may wear more than one set of clothing on a regular Sunday morning. His garments may change either because he has preached in them or they are wet or for some other reason. When there is more than one change of clothing, these should also be inspected prior to the pastor's dressing in them. If your pastor has several garments that he may wear on a regular Sunday, these garments must be pressed, cleared of all lint and the buttons loosed, in preparation for quick robing or dressing when your pastor needs them.

Be sure that you know each garment, the difference between each garment and the significance of the garments so that you will know what is appropriate for each environment in which your pastor ministers. Some of the most common garments are explained and defined in the Appendix section at the end of the book.

The garments that your pastor wears are **sacred**. They should not be regarded simply as items of clothing. They represent various aspects of God's nature and they should be valued for the spiritual importance, and they should be cared for with reverence. When they are being carried by Armorbearers, they should not be dragged or allowed to touch the floor. These items should be dry cleaned on a regular basis when necessary and carefully stored when they are not in use.

D. SERVING THE SENIOR PASTOR

Control the environment around the pastor: When the pastor arrives for service, he really does not care to be involved in a lot of conversation. He is usually in a reflective mood, making himself available to be used by God for the day's assignment. Armorbearers are therefore expected to aid the pastor in this desire by curtailing the access to him and allowing him the free time to commune with God.

Persons who desire to see the pastor should be encouraged to make an appointment or to wait until the service is completed. If the matter is purported to be urgent, the Armorbearer should take a message and forward it to the pastor or the executive pastor for a decision to be made as to whether the pastor will receive that visitor. Unless given specific instructions on this matter, an Armorbearer should not take it upon himself to deny or approve access to the pastor. Depending on the severity of the situation, asking the assistance of an executive pastor is always a safe option.

The pastor's office is not a place for chit-chat. Armorbearers should remain quiet and alert at all times. Even though they are alert and attentive to the environment around them, they should be in a prayerful attitude for the pastor and the service. Stay alert at all times (don't find yourself doing errands for other people).

Prepare items for the pulpit: The interior armorbearer should prepare the items for the pulpit as well as coffee or the beverage of choice and have them available for the pastor's consumption on his arrival. If the pastor takes vitamins or other medications and has granted permissions to you, these should be set out for him.

Escort to the pulpit: Once the pastor is ready to enter the Sanctuary for service, the Armorbearer escorts the pastor to the pulpit, one in front of him and the other behind him. One armorbearer is leading and directing and the other is protecting. This allows the pastor to move directly to the pulpit without being distracted or drawn from his assignment to share the Word of God with the people of God. As you serve here, be sure not to overcrowd the pastor.

Serving during service: When the Armorbearers and pastor arrive on the pulpit, they are seated after the pastor sits. At this time, the Armorbearer serves with a prayerful spirit. He is alert, watching for any activity that would warrant his reaction, for example a request for the announcement folder, Bible, preaching notes, or a request to get something from his office. The Armorbearer should know the order of service and keep a watchful eye on both the pastor and the first assistant. In so doing, he will be aware of what is happening next in the service and can prepare himself to serve. Sometimes the pastor changes the procedure and so Armorbearers should be watching and listening so that they can adapt to the changes without delay.

When the introduction is made for the preacher, choose an appropriate time, when it will be least distracting, to put his Bible, preaching notes and a towel on the altar. Pour a glass of water or whatever beverage he drinks and place it in the designated place. This drink should be at room temperature unless otherwise requested. If your pastor has another preference as to when the drink should be poured, then that is the protocol that should be followed.

During the service, Armorbearers should be seated where they can have easy access to the pastor and to the pastor's office. The male Armorbearers on duty are required to keep a watchful eye on the pastor, first assistant and the Armorbearers working the pulpit for any signals they may give. This allows the team to work together smoothly and to accomplish necessary tasks without being a distraction to the pastor and others in the service.

When the pastor moves among the crowd, Armorbearers move with him at a distance so that they do not crowd him but are watchful of the activities of the people around him. They are always ready to protect should the need arise. Exercising a discerning spirit is very important at this point, because there is only a small window of opportunity to decide what is an attack or just an overrated greeting.

At the end of the sermon when the pastor is about to minister, the Armorbearer prepares to place the cape or other garment used on the pastor. While in a prepared position, watch for the ready signal. If he does not give a signal, move to the area just behind him to put the cape on before or after the benediction. Then proceed to a location that you can move towards the exit door where he is likely to go after the benediction. Ensure you have a throat lozenge for the pastor to give him immediate relief after the sermon. Do this discreetly.

At the door, watch both the pastor and the parishioner leaving in case the need for your service arises. If a parishioner gives something to your pastor, once he has moved, you should take this item from your pastor so that his hands are free to greet other members. These items should be placed in the pastor's office so that he can take further action at a later time. While one Armorbearer is at the door with the pastor, another one should clear the altar, taking away the Bible, preaching notes and other items that were used.

When the pastor has completed greeting the parishioners, keep a keen eye on the direction he takes and escort him to his destination. At the end of the final service, all clothing used will be given to the chauffer or placed in his car for return home. All dishes used will be washed and placed in their appropriate places, leaving the kitchenette clean.

The service of the Armorbearer is completed once the pastor leaves the premises. If for any reason the pastor remains on-site after a service, Armorbearers should remain available for service. Once the pastor leaves, the Armorbearers are free to leave as well.

CHAPTER FIVE

PREPARING TO SERVE
AT HOME

—⚭—

Now that you have prepared for and received your pastor, let's get set to serve for a regular Sunday service or conference at your church.

Serving your pastor in your local assembly is one of the best places in which you can get your practice. Because the environment is familiar and you have the opportunity to serve often, this is the time for you to develop the characteristics and attitudes that will help you to excel in your service if you travel with your pastor. Serving often allows you to get on the job training and exposure to different situations so that when you go on the road you can minimize mistakes. I want to advise you, then, not to take serving in your local church lightly.

Every time you have the opportunity to serve, approach it with the intent of developing your skills and also as a time to get to know your pastor better—what his likes and dislikes are. As you get this information, do all you can to improve yourself and your service.

In this chapter, we will cover various aspects of serving as an Armorbearer including serving during service, serving on the altar, serving during ministry time, serving guest speakers and serving at official functions. Here are some practical pointers for serving well in your home church.

A. SERVING AT REGULAR SUNDAY SERVICES

Check the schedule to find out which service and in what capacity you will be working:
If your church has more than one Armorbearer, there should be a schedule or a roster in place that outlines who will serve, when they serve and in what capacity they will be serving. This is especially important if your church has multiple services. Once you find out the time you will be serving and you know what area you will be serving in, then you should make sure that you do what is necessary to prepare yourself. This may include asking questions, being observant or placing yourself in the position to receive the information you need for your assignment. To do this, you should show up at least 45 minutes prior to the start of the service.

Upon arrival, check in at the pastor's office to see if there are any last minute changes: Things change. Instructions change. There is more than one way to achieve a desired result. I want to emphasize this point because the pastor you serve moves by the Spirit. He may have intended to do one thing, planned to do one thing and then, on the command of the Holy Spirit, he may change plans. As an Armorbearer, you cannot afford to be caught off guard by a major change in plans. Also, some things cannot be planned and have to be "played by ear." Since this is a regular occurrence in the environment you serve in, check and re-check to make sure you have the latest and most current information you need to properly execute your assignment.

Ensure that the office is kept clear and quiet at all times: Whatever the cost, make sure that you do not allow your pastor's office to become a marketplace. Make sure you keep it clear and quiet at all times. Your Pastor is preparing to minister the Word of God, and the environment around his office should be one of reverence. There should not be a lot of conversations, joke telling, recapping the latest news events or even singing close to the pastor's office, even among other Armorbearers. This can be very distracting to the pastor who is getting ready to preach. You are responsible to maintain an environment for your pastor that allows him the quiet time to meditate and prepare for service.

Let me help here. I know your question to me now is, "How can I do this when the people who are making the noise or causing the distraction are senior members and officers of the ministry? How can I tell the church administrator not to be so loud while passing the pastor's office?" Before I answer that, let me lay a few misconceptions aside about your role as an Armorbearer, and then I will answer that question for you. As an Armorbearer, your sole responsibility is to your pastor and his family. In performing your job, you will have to do some things and say some things that will cause other people to hate you. You cannot be consumed by that. You have been appointed to serve, and you must do what you must to complete the assignment that you have been given. Now to answer your question. In fulfilling your mandate, if you have to tell a senior member, or any member for that matter, not to do something, do it with respect and with grace. How you speak to them should be as important as what you say. Simply say, "Ma'am, the pastor is preparing to minister right now and your conversation is a little distracting." Or you may say, "Can you kindly continue your conversation at a further distance? Thank you for your cooperation."

Now be warned, even with all the grace and all of the respect you may use, there may still be some who will be offended by your actions and take exception to you. They may feel that you are keeping them from their pastor or that you have no right to deny them access. In these cases, do the best you can and leave the rest to be resolved at a later time. Stay firm to your responsibility, though, to control the environment around your pastor, whatever the cost.

B. SERVING ON THE ALTAR

The Armorbearer who is serving directly with the pastor should make sure that the following items are prepared. These will be kept on a table in a bag or a basket for use by the pastor or others so designated during a service. It should probably contain the following general items:

- Water
- Juice
- A beverage glass for each person to be served
- Coasters
- Glass Covers
- Lozenges
- Napkins
- A box of Kleenex
- A tray with writing paper and pen
- Note cards
- Tithers envelope
- Service bulletin

The Armorbearer should ensure that adequate amounts of these items are available for use before, during and after the sermon. Once you have mounted the pulpit, you should not have to move to replenish these items as that could create a distraction. In addition to these general items, the following personal items should be taken with you when you escort the pastor out to the pulpit.

- Towels (3) wrapped in tissue or plastic
- Announcements folder
- The sermon notes

- Outer garment for use during ministry time or after the sermon
- Anything that is particular to your pastor's needs

The towels you pack to be used during service should coordinate with the colors of the garment your pastor is wearing. This gives a better impression than if they were not color-coordinated. The towels should be wrapped in plastic or hand towels to avoid excess dirt or direct contact by the Armorbearer. These items will be used by your pastor to wipe his face and they should be handled with the utmost care and attention. As a matter of fact, you should prepare a bag or appropriate container to carry the towels and hand-kerchiefs. Once they have been used, they should be sent home to be cleaned and properly stored for future use. You should not take any of your pastor's personal items home with you, even to be washed. Taking official garments to the cleaners to be cleaned is acceptable.

The Armorbearer who is serving on the pulpit should be aware of the time in the service when the Announcements folder and the sermon notes will be required by the pastor so that they can be provided at the appropriate time and not delay the service. They should be easily accessible to the pastor as well in case they want to review them before they use them at the pulpit. You should remain alert so that you can respond quickly if the pastor needs something else from you during service.

Maintain eye contact: Observation skills are very important while serving in ministry. You must always be aware of what is going on around you. In my first book, *DEVELOPING A HEART FOR SERVICE*, I spoke about observation, anticipation and taking action. You not only need to be aware of what is going on around you, but you must also be able to keep your eyes on your pastor and others who are serving with you.

One of the things you should never do on the Pulpit is get too relaxed. Sit upright and always be ready to move. You should study your pastor so well that you learn his body or sign language. Stay alert, anticipate and be ready for action at all times. Do not become a sleeping, gazing and carefree armorbearer.

Communication on the pulpit: If you or someone else needs to communicate with your pastor while he is on the pulpit, do not interrupt him if his eyes are closed. He may be meditating or hearing from God. In either case, your interruption is inappropriate. Write your message on a message card (an example is shown in the Appendix) and place it on the table next to your pastor. Do not pass messages to your pastor on pieces of paper or torn bulletins. This is disrespectful. Have message cards prepared and use them instead. When your pastor notices the message card on the table, he will read it and respond to it. At that time, you can convey his message to the relevant party. If he does not respond to it, then do not press him. When he is about to minister, he is not always interested in too much talking. Give him that respect.

As far as possible, try to keep outside communication to the pastor at a minimum once he is on the pulpit. These can become distractions. This is especially the case when the matter for concern cannot be immediately addressed by him. If you have been so empowered, scan the messages before passing them on so that you do not disrupt the pastor unnecessarily. If you do receive messages that do not require an immediate response, hold them until after the service and them pass them on. If you are not sure, pass it in to the first assistant or executive pastor for action.

At the end of the sermon, throat lozenges and room temperature water/juice should be made available. Also the pastor should be covered (usually a cape) to protect his health. During this time you should be watchful for those persons who may want to lay hands on the pastor or get close to him after he is done preaching. This can be very dangerous.

When you serve on the pulpit, you should be very prayerful and maintain a spirit of worship. You should speak only if asked a question and you should try to limit your movement so that you are not a distraction. The pulpit is not a show or a runway. A quiet and prayerful disposition is your most valuable asset serving in this position.

C. SERVING DURING MINISTRY TIME

When your pastor is moving, keep the pathway clear in front of him: As an armorbearer you must always appear to be kind but firm. Whenever your pastor is headed to the pulpit or the floor or wherever you are taking him, make sure you lead him and keep the path clear. You also want to make sure you keep glancing over your shoulder so as not to leave him far behind. This will help you also to be aware if he has stopped or was diverted for any reason.

Protect your pastor at all times: Just as the woman with the issue of blood was able to draw from Jesus to be healed, in the same way others can pass on demonic spirits during this time because the pastor may be physically weak after preaching or ministering at the altar. Your spirit of discernment must kick in to give you more direction as to how close you should serve during this time.

Do not become a hindrance during ministry: Even though the pastor may be under a heavy anointing, he is aware of his surroundings. Don't hold him back or try to stop him unless he appears to be endangering himself or if another pastor gives an indication.

Do not overcrowd the pastor: Protect the pastor at all times, but do not overcrowd him. As you serve, you must be sure to give enough room for him to move. Observe who he is praying for, and be aware of the other people around him but do not try to hinder the work of ministry trying to protect him. Be sensitive.

Armorbearers should not try to prevent members from reaching him, especially at the door after service or the established place where they greet him. Give your pastor enough space to greet and fellowship with his members.

Unless you are praying for him, try to be as alert as possible during ministry time. There is a lot at stake and you should be prepared to move quickly if the need arises.

D. SERVING GUEST MINISTERS

When Solomon had guests at the temple, he pulled out all of the stops. Your pastor has the same desire and Armorbearers have a role to play in giving excellent service to those who are guests of the ministry. We will use the Biblical example of Solomon to show you how.

Now when the queen of Sheba heard of the fame of Solomon concerning the name of the LORD, she came to test him with hard questions. She came to Jerusalem with a very great retinue, with camels that bore spices, very much gold, and precious stones; and when she came to Solomon, she spoke with him about all that was in her heart. So Solomon answered all her questions; there was nothing so difficult for the king that he could not explain it to her. And when the queen of Sheba had seen all the wisdom of Solomon, the house that he had built, the food on his table, the seating of his servants, the service of his waiters and their apparel, his cupbearers, and the entryway by which he went up to the house of the LORD, there was no more spirit in her. Then she said to the king: "It was a true report which I heard in my own land about your words and your wisdom. However I did not believe the words until I came and saw with my own eyes; and indeed the half was not told me. Your wisdom and prosperity exceed the fame of which I heard. Happy are your men and happy are these your servants, who stand continually before you and hear your wisdom! Blessed be the LORD your God, who delighted in you, setting you on the throne of Israel! Because the LORD has loved Israel forever, therefore He made you king, to do justice and righteousness." Then she gave the king one hundred and twenty talents of gold, spices in great quantity, and precious stones. There never again came such abundance of spices as the queen of Sheba gave to King Solomon.

1 Kings 10:1-10

Remember, the Queen of Sheba was amazed at the level of service of King Solomon's attendants to the point where she fainted. You should seek to give the same experience to your pastor's guest. Here are a few ways:

Armorbearers should arrive at the service at least 45 minutes before the scheduled time. You should check in at the office and with the first assistant to find out the following information:

i. The name of the guest speaker
ii. The time they are expected to arrive at the sanctuary
iii. Whether his or her spouse and/or children are with him or her
iv. Whether his or her armorbearer is with him or her
v. The number of people accompanying the speaker (if a group)
vi. Whether or not products are for sale

You should know the name of the guest speaker so that you can address him or her properly when you give your greeting. Be especially familiar with ecclesiastical titles (Bishop, Overseer, Pastor, Minister, etc.). This is even more critical if the guest is not a member of your denomination. You want to be very careful not to offend the guest by addressing him or her improperly.

Prior to the arrival of the guest, the Armorbearer should know where the guest will be seated. If a spouse and family are attending the service also, they should know where they will sit so that on arrival he or she can be escorted directly to his or her seat without being delayed. If a group is accompanying the guest, they are cared for by the church's hospitality or protocol ministry. It is customary that seats will be reserved for them as well.

Arrival: Once you know the expected time of arrival of the guest speaker, move to the receiving area where he or she will be dropped off. When the speaker arrives, open the door for him or her and extend your hand in greeting, introducing yourself so that the guest knows who you are. Do not initiate any further conversation unless the guest initiates it. At this time, you should give instructions to the guest as confirmed with the church office. This includes whether the guest speaker will be escorted directly into the service or will meet the pastor first before entering the sanctuary. Whatever is the case, the Armorbearer will escort the guest to the designated place. If the guest is carrying items, you should offer to assist. If he or she has questions, you should be in a position to respond or to find the information and relay it if the requested information that is not readily available to you.

Inform the pastor of the arrival of the guest speaker. When the pastor comes to greet the speaker, leave the room, closing the door behind you, allowing them some private time. Remain near the door to hear when the pastor is ready to go into the sanctuary or have you do something for him or his guest.

Serving the guest speaker: If the guest speaker is not accompanied by an Armorbearer, then one should be assigned to him or her. Armorbearers serve guest speakers in the same manner in which they would serve their senior pastors. After all, they are your pastor's guests. Please see the section on "Serving the Senior Pastor" in Chapter 4 for a recap of this information.

The same Armorbearer who greets the guest on his arrival should be the same one who will work with him or her for the duration of their stay (if they are speaking for more than one service). This makes it easier for the guests who will only have to remember one person and also provides for better service since his or her preferences and requests will not have to be repeated to others who serve them.

The Armorbearers who are serving the guests should find out their preferences in what they would like to drink and when to be sure that those items are available. When guests come to the ministry, usually they send in a comfort assistance form (one is attached in the Appendix) that gives this information. You should be aware of these items and be sure that if they are not on hand that they are obtained prior to the arrival of the Guest.

Hosting Armorbearers: If the guest speakers bring Armorbearers with them, you should allow their Armorbearers to serve them. Introduce yourself to the Armorbearers and then work along with them to give them information about things peculiar to your ministry or to assist with items they may need but do not have. Your role will be to host the Armorbearers who are serving their pastors. For example, making tea or other tasks that require the resources of your ministry, you should offer to perform since you are familiar with the environment. You should offer to secure the garments of the guest speakers where they will be safe and accessible after the ministry time and then do so. In hosting Armorbearers, any question you have for the guests, you should direct to them and allow your guests to stay focused on their assignment.

When escorting the pastor and guest speaker to the pulpit, the local Armorbearer leads, with the senior pastor next, followed by the guest speaker and his Armorbearer. The guest Armorbearer serves while on the pulpit. This includes putting his pastor's Bible and preaching notes on the altar. When the guest is finished preaching, at his decision, the local Armorbearer escorts him or her back to the office to change. If the guest is a male, a male Armorbearer assigned will accompany him into the green room. When there is no Armorbearer with the guest preacher, a local Armorbearer is assigned to him or her specifically, and another Armorbearer serves the senior pastor exclusively.

If the guest speaker brought products and materials to be sold, the Armorbearer should have a member of the media sales team come to assist the guests with information on how this process works in the church and where his materials can be set up. It is important to note that the Armorbearer only makes the introductions for this process. He does not become involved in the process and should not be distracted from his primary responsibility to serve the guest.

If there are after service functions, the Armorbearers assigned will remain and be ready to serve until the guests leave the premises. As a host, you should try to make the stay of your guests as comfortable as possible. They should be handled with the same care and respect as your pastor.

E. SERVING AT OFFICIAL FUNCTIONS

There may be occasions when official services may be conducted at your local church. Official services may refer to ecumenical activities such as ordinations, consecrations or other such services. Official services may also be official state visits of the president, prime minister or other national services. In these services, the role of the Armorbearer becomes very visible, and it is extremely important that his service is properly executed.

- **If you are scheduled for a special ceremony or service, be sure to find out the nature of the service and any special requests or instructions.**

The first step to preparing to serve at official functions is to know the nature of the service. Perhaps of even greater importance is what role is your senior pastor playing in the event. Is he being honored? Is he hosting the event? Is he simply an invited guest? Obviously, if your pastor is hosting the event, more is required of the Armorbearer than if the pastor were simply a guest at the function. If your pastor is hosting the event, then all of the special guests should be attended to in the manner described in the previous section entitled, "Serving Guest Speakers." There should be a group of Armorbearers assigned to the guest speakers of the service and to attend to their special needs. Protocol officers will also play a key role here.

- **Make sure you are clear about what you are expected to do before, during and after the service.**

According to the nature of the service and the role your pastor is playing, the level of involvement of Armorbearers will vary. Make sure that you are properly informed as to what your responsibilities are during the function. Find out if there will be other bishops, pastors or government officials present and who will be serving them. Be able to act quickly—don't get too relaxed or jammed in during these services, as you may be needed on the spur of the moment. Be prepared to act in case dignitaries and special guests show up unannounced, and get a directive from your pastor as to what you should do if this happens. That way you will not offend any special guests, and you will know how your pastor would want them to be handled.

Having a copy of the programme beforehand is also helpful as you will have an idea of the length of the service and those who will take part in it. Even though the Programme will give you a better understanding of how you can serve, still follow up to see if there has been last-minute changes.

CHAPTER SIX

PREPARING TO SERVE
ON THE ROAD

—ɯ—

" Serving on the Road" refers to the times in which your pastor ministers or preaches outside of your church. Whether he preaches at the church next door or a church in another city, state, or country, he is "serving on the road." When this happens, the role of the Armorbearer in serving and protecting his pastor becomes extremely important as he is serving in unfamiliar territory. Finding out as much information as you can about the engagement and preparing yourself in advance will make a significant impact on whether you are successful in your assignment.

Armorbearers who serve with the pastor when he ministers away from the local congregation should be at the service site at least 45 minutes prior to the time the service is to begin. On your arrival to the ministry site, find a representative of the ministry you are visiting and identify yourself so that you can receive any last minute information or changes as it relates to the service. Prior to the engagement, the Armorbearer should find out:

i. The name of the pastor and his spouse
ii. The name of the church/ministry
iii. The location where the service will be held
iv. The scheduled time of the service
v. The type of service (regular service, conference, consecration, etc.)
vi. The type of official garments to be worn by the pastor.

This information may be obtained from your church's office, and if it is not available there, it should be obtained from the host church.

Armorbearers should find out the proper pronunciation and spelling of the host pastor's name. The proper manner in which the pastor is to be addressed in also important (Bishop, Overseer, Reverend, etc.). This information is important to know in case you are asked. You should also find out the name of the pastor's spouse and his children so that you can pass this information on to your pastor.

Armorbearers should know the name of the church or ministry that your pastor is going to. Use the Internet or other resources to find out as much information on the ministry as you can. Having this information in hand will cause you to be more prepared for serving than having no information at all.

Armorbearers should know the location of the engagement site so that they can be there 45 minutes prior to the service time. Some time before the actual engagement, Armorbearers should travel to the site first of all to know where it is and secondly to make a cursory inspection of the site. This will help them to take note of any special circumstances or situations that may be of importance to the pastor. For example, if it is a small church with no changing room, that information will impact whether or not the pastor will arrive to the service already dressed to minister.

The type of service will, in most cases, dictate the garments that will be worn by the pastor. These garments should be prepared and retrieved from the church by the Armorbearer. In addition to this, having this information will give the Armorbearer some idea of the kind of preparation he needs to make in order to properly serve his Pastor.

A. SERVING AT SPEAKING ENGAGEMENTS (Local)

Armorbearers who serve with pastors when they minister away from the local congregation should be at the service site at least 45 minutes prior to the time the service is to begin. On your arrival to the ministry site, find a representative of the ministry you are visiting and identify yourself so that you can receive any last minute information or changes as it relates to the service. When you arrive at the site, you should do the following:

i. Find out where the pastor will park.
ii. Get a copy of the service programme.
iii. Fill in the engagement information form (or at least know the answers).
iv. Find out whether he will be taken directly into the service.
v. See if there is a holding room/office for changing or meditation time.
vi. Secure a seat for the pastor's spouse.
vii. Check with the pastor or his assistant for any last minute changes.
viii. Find out the location where the sale of ministry products will take place

Parking – Ensure that there has been a designated place for the pastor to park. There should be clear access into and out of the space in the event the pastor chooses to leave right after the ministry time. After a powerful time of ministry, pastors get weak, tired and drained. If your pastor's car is blocked in or he gets caught up in a traffic congestion trying to leave the service, this can be detrimental at worst and frustrating at the least. Securing the parking space can alleviate this situation.

Programme – Once you arrive at the engagement site, secure a copy of the programme. Find out how far along in the service your pastor will make his presentation and inform him. If the service starts before your pastor arrives, keep him updated as to the progress of the service so that he can be prepared once he arrives to take the next course of action necessary. Use the programme to help you complete the Engagement Information Form (shown in the Appendix).

Engagement Information Form – See the Engagement Information Form in the Appendix of the book and fill in the required information so that your pastor can make the proper acknowledgments when he makes his introductory remarks. This is part of your preparation for your assignment, and it will make your pastor more effective in his assignment.

Changing and Green Room – When you arrive, find out whether a place has been designated for your pastor to robe and prepare for the service or to change his clothing after the service. If there is no such provision, communicate this information to your pastor so that he can arrive prepared and already robed or dressed for service.

Seating – Ensure that proper seating arrangements have been made for the pastor's family if they will be accompanying him to the service. If they are present in the service and your pastor cannot see them, this may cause him to be uncomfortable, especially in an unfamiliar environment. The seating for the pastor's family should be on the front row or in a place where they are clearly visible to the pastor as they deliver the Word of God.

Post Service Functions – If the pastor remains for after-service functions, Armorbearers remain to ensure that they cover their pastors. Once the pastor leaves, then Armorbearers are free to do the same.

B. TRAVELING WITH THE SENIOR PASTOR

Traveling with your pastor to an engagement is an honor. It is not a free trip for you to go shopping, rest or to have vacation. It is a working trip. Armorbearers have to especially guard against a lethargic or a lazy spirit when traveling engagements arise. You have to guard against the tendency to be so relaxed that you do not serve your pastor with excellence. If your pastor is trying to reach you to complete some last minute details before his ministry, you should not be out in the pool or in the spa having a relaxing time! That is not the purpose of your trip. You should not be out on some personal shopping spree, but you should be preparing yourself for service. While traveling with your pastor, you should be helping, lifting and supporting him in his ministry assignment. Please serve with this in mind so that you do not aggravate his spirit before he executes his ministry assignment.

As you travel, do not wear your pastor out and do not allow others to do it. Traveling for ministry is usually very taxing physically, and he needs to maintain his strength and energy. Be sensitive and help him to preserve these quiet moments for reflection and meditation.

If you are traveling with your pastor to an international engagement or an engagement that is away from your local city or state, the following five areas should be given special attention by the Armorbearer. They are presented in point form for ease of reference.

1. The Day before Travel
2. At the Airport

3. At the Hotel
4. At the Engagement Site
5. Post-service Functions

BEFORE TRAVEL DAY

● Make contact with the ministry liaison from the local church. Introduce yourself and become acquainted so that you can ensure that all of your pastor's needs for the trip can be met adequately. If for some reason the host church is not able to fulfill some of the requirements, then the Armorbearer should take measures to ensure that he can meet these needs on his own.

● Review the event information with the host church or the person who arranged your pastor's travel before the travel day. Re-check the time of the event and the time that you will be picked up from the hotel and transported to the Engagement site. Check the expected dress code of the event. (See Travel Profile in the Appendix.)

● Verify any changes to the event scheduling prior to travel. Sometimes there may be changes to the event since the time your pastor accepted the invitation.

● If you can, secure a copy of the programme for the service/event so that you can properly prepare. You do not want to be surprised or unprepared for any situation. For example, maybe the engagement calls for ceremonial dress and your pastor did not bring the proper garment because he was not aware. This is not the position you want your pastor to be in. Ask enough questions to ensure that you are adequately prepared to serve.

- Become familiar with the host church and the event being hosted. Use the church's website or information obtained directly from the ministry to familiarize yourself with the ministry. You should not show up to the engagement with "absolutely no idea" of where you are going. This shows lack of preparation. Do sufficient research so that you are at least a little familiar with the ministry.

- Research the city, state or country of the engagement site. Give your pastor the information you find so that he too can be informed. Look for economic, social and religious information about the area and be aware of current events. This information makes for good conversation once you and your pastor are on-site. It also makes you appear informed, and you will make your pastor look good by such preparation. Further, you will be well received by your guests by showing interest in his ministry.

- Find out if there will be after-service functions.

- Ensure that all ministry materials and products for sale are packed (Cassettes/CD/DVDs). A price list should be included together with a full inventory of products for easy record-keeping and accounting once the engagement is completed.

- Be sensitive with your pastor's travel information. It is not everybody's business. This information should be kept private and confidential.

- Review your travel itinerary and note the times of layover and connecting flights so that you can have this information fresh in your mind.

- Ensure that you have per diem monies for tips, taxis and bellman so that your pastor does not have to pay for any of these services.

- Secure the phone number for the pastor of the church, the driver or the protocol officer who will be picking you up from the airport. Be sure to have the address of the hotel and a confirmation number for the reservations in case you have to make your own transportation arrangements for some reason.

TRAVEL DAY

- Arrive early at the airport for check-in. Do not be late. Your pastor should not have to wait for you. You should be at the airport waiting to receive your pastor when he arrives and help him with the check-in process.

- Travel light so that you can help your pastor with his travel items.

- Have the information sheet that details movements so that you can be prepared to serve. What is the duration of the trip? What is the service time? How far is the engagement site from the hotel? What time will your pastor be leaving the hotel to get to the engagement site?

- Physical demands of travel make your pastor tired and easily irritable. You should be prepared to serve keeping this in mind. Don't ask too many questions. These are your pastor's final moments to prepare for the assignment and he is usually in a meditative mood. You can engage conversation if he does but if he does not, remain alert so that you can guard these final moments of preparation from other disruptions.

- Once you have arrived at the destination airport or station, meet the receiving party and introduce yourself. Ensure that they are ready to receive your pastor by bringing the transportation up to the loading door.

- Escort your pastor to the transportation provided so that he can relax.

- Check for luggage and ensure that all pieces are collected. If a skycap service is used, be sure to tip for transferring the luggage to the waiting car.

- After hotel check-in, escort your pastor to his room. Make sure he knows your room number and how he can contact you if the need arises.

GETTING READY FOR THE ENGAGEMENT

- Make sure that the pastor's garments are prepared (pressed and ironed if necessary).

- Coordinate the time your pastor will be transported to the engagement. Confirm the pick-up time with your pastor so that he is aware.

- Confirm with the host the time your pastor is expected to get up to preach and coordinate his arrival time to the service. Be aware of time changes (EST, Pacific time, etc.).

- Your travel bag should always be packed (glass, drinks, lozenges, sermon notes, towels and juices).

- Once the time is set, you should report to the lobby of the hotel at least 15 minutes prior to the pick-up time. Your pastor will probably not leave his room until the transportation has arrived. It is better for him to wait restfully in his room than down in the lobby.

- At the pick-up time, if the transportation has not yet arrived, call your pastor in his room and give him a status report. Let him know if the transportation is there, if they will be late or some other changes have been made.

- When your pastor arrives in the lobby, take a cursory inspection of his clothing. Ensure that buttons are done, zippers are fastened, no creases or mashes are evident, and that no lint is noticeable on his suit. Since first impressions are important, you want to be sure that everything is in order. If something is out of place, mention it to him in the event he wants to return to his room to fix it. Do not wait until he cannot correct a problem to bring it to his attention.

- Once you have been picked up, if you are allowed to, sit in the front seat with the driver. This allows you to control the atmosphere in the car on the way to the engagement. If your pastor does not like to talk much before preaching, you should ensure that the driver is not being excessively talkative. If the air conditioning affects your pastor, make sure that it is at a comfortable level. Since your pastor is most likely to be in a meditative mood, make sure that if music is being played, that it is not inappropriate and that it is not too loud. Be creative and try to preserve the sanctity of the moment. If you are not able to sit in the front seat, try to carry out these functions from wherever you are seated as best as you can.

● Once you arrive at the engagement site, escort your pastor to the green room or changing room if there is one and store his garment bag which contains his change of clothes for after the service. As much as possible, be sure that you are the one to handle your pastor's garments. This is for personal as well as spiritual reasons. Once the garments have been stored, excuse yourself from the room so that your pastor can make final preparations for ministry.

SERVING AT THE ENGAGEMENT

● Introduce yourself to the host Armorbearer assigned to your pastor and confirm with him that he can liaise with you about any questions he may have.

● If you are traveling with your pastor as an Armorbearer, then you should serve as the Armorbearer. The local Armorbearer does not know your pastor the way that you do. You should be the one who serves him while the local Armorbearer assists you in areas that you are not familiar with as it relates to the local church and its protocols.

● Along with the local Armorbearer, review the pulpit layout and find out where your pastor will sit when he comes out into the service. Find out where you will sit so that as you escort your pastor, you know exactly where you are going.

- Along with the local Armorbearer, deliver the ministry products to the assigned place where they will be sold. Have a brief conversation with the ministry staff that will facilitate the sale of those products and ensure that you address any questions they may have. Present the Price List and the Inventory Product List to assist them in their service. Keep a set of any items that will be promoted from the pulpit or list them on the Engagement Form (see Appendix).

- Find out the time in the service when your pastor will mount the pulpit so that you can place his Bible and notes on the altar at the proper time.

- Understand the cues of your pastor so that you can serve well. What do they do to indicate that the sound is not right or something is wrong? Know your pastor's needs and how you can attend to them without them having to SAY something.

- Keep your pastor in view at all times. Do not become so caught up in the message or the service that you do not recognize a need he may have.

- As you keep your pastor in view, observe your surroundings. Remember, the Armorbearer is responsible for protecting the pastor. You can do this more effectively if you are aware of everything that is going on in your immediate vicinity.

- Serve your pastor as you would normally in your home church. Put up his Bible, sermon notes, towels and drink as you would if you were serving in your home church.

- Be prayerful as the sermon is being delivered and intercede for the anointing of God, the power of God and for clarity in its delivery.

- Be professional and courteous at all times. Remember that you represent your pastor and the way you serve is a reflection of his character.

- Remember that each church has its own protocols that may be different from yours. Your behaviour should be in order and custom of the ministry that you are serving in as far as possible.

SERVING AFTER THE ENGAGEMENT

- Prior to the ministry time, find out from the host Armorbearer if there will be after-service dining or whether you will be free to leave the engagement site after the service. Communicate this information to your pastor.

- Once your pastor has completed his ministry, escort him to the green room or holding room. Do not enter the room unless you have been invited to do so. Remain near the door of the room in the event that he needs you do something or to get something for him.

- Once your pastor has changed his garments, secure them as you would if you were at home and pack them properly (wet items into a plastic bag).

- Once the changed garments are packed, take the garment bag to the car that will transport you back to the hotel (if it is nearby), or alternatively ensure that they are properly secured. Be sure not to leave any items behind.

● Ensure that your pastor is comfortable where he is, whether at the after-service dining or meeting with congregants, before you become involved in other activities.

● Find out from your pastor if he will go to the product table to sign autographs or greet the members. If he is, escort him to the designated location.

● Observe your pastor carefully as he moves after the ministry time. Note his level of energy and vulnerability. If you think that these levels are low, encourage him to retire early. Sometimes pastors do not recognize how tired they are or how much energy they used to deliver the message.

● If your pastor has to retire early, you may advise those who are working with you that he is unable to continue. You may give an explanation that will help the patrons to understand the reason for his early departure. Remember your role to make him look good.

● If your pastor remains for the after-service dining, you should allow him the privacy to share with the hosts. If such provision has not been made, request of the hosts that you will eat at a table away from your pastor to give him this privilege. During this time, be sure to maintain eye contact with your pastor in the event that your service is required.

- Be sure to collect all funds and remaining products for return with you. If you have made alternate arrangements with the host ministry in this regard, make sure to follow up with them so that you can give a full report to your pastor when he enquires.

- Request a copy of the message given by your pastor. After every engagement, you should secure a copy of the sermon/presentation for your pastor's records.

RETURN TRAVEL

- Find out what arrangements have been made, if any, for your transportation to the airport by the host church.

- If the host church did not make any arrangements for you to get to the airport, make them yourself.

- Inform your pastor as to the arrangements that have been made and the time for the departure from the hotel.

- Do not oversleep. Set the alarm. Call the front desk. Sleep with the lights on. Do whatever you need to do so that you do not oversleep. You should be awake in sufficient time to get yourself ready and give a wake up call to your pastor.

- Once you are dressed and ready, check out of your room and deliver your luggage to the lobby. As you prepare to check out, give your pastor a second call to be sure that he is up and mobilized.

- Once you have checked out, find out if your pastor needs any assistance in having his luggage brought down from the room. If there is a need, send a bellman. Be sure to tip the bellman.

- As he enters the lobby, offer to check him out so that he can proceed directly to the transportation.

- Coordinate with the skycap for luggage transport to the counter at the airport. Assist with the check-in process as you did when you originated on the trip.

- Once the check-in process is complete, offer to get something for your pastor to eat and drink so that he does not have to stand in long lines at the airport.

- As he relaxes and initiates conversation, recap the ministry experience with your pastor. Share with him anything of concern to you and allow him to help you to sharpen your skills for the next traveling engagement. Each opportunity should help you to serve better the next time around. If he does not initiate conversation, either because he is weary or unwilling, you can recap with him at a later time when you return home.

- Once you arrive home, assist your pastor in retrieving his luggage and any other airport clearance procedures.

- Once the luggage has been retrieved, arrange with the skycap or other airport personnel to have the items transported to the outside. The tip should be covered from your per diem or from your own resources.

- Ensure that your pastor is escorted into his transportation before you leave him. If his car is not there for some reason, you should wait with him. If this becomes a long time of waiting, find out whether he would like you to secure some alternate means of transportation to get home. If it is okay, then secure a taxi or other transportation for him.

- Once the pastor leaves the airport, your assignment is completed and you are free to leave.

CHAPTER SEVEN

PREPARING TO SERVE AFTER SERVICE

—ɯᴠ—

A. POST SERVICE FUNCTIONS

There are three types of after-service functions that will be covered to highlight the role Armorbearers play in various situations:

    I. No after-service meal
    II. Light refreshments
    III. Dinner

NO AFTER-SERVICE MEAL

Home: If no meal is offered after service when you serve at home, then you should serve in the same manner that you do regularly. Assist your pastor, if required, in his after-service tasks as needed. Once your pastor leaves the church, you are free to leave.

On the Road: If there is no meal served after service, your pastor may still spend time talking with the host pastor. If this happens, give them enough room to speak to each other privately. You should proceed to secure the garment bags and other materials so that once your pastor is done conversing, you can leave the premises. Even if you will not have a meal at the engagement site, you should at least ensure that your pastor has something to drink to replenish himself until he can have something to eat. Once you are in transit from the engagement site, find out from your pastor if he would like to stop somewhere to have dinner or whether he will order room service from the hotel. Find out this information in sufficient time to ensure that you can make whatever arrangements are necessary to make it happen.

LIGHT REFRESHMENTS

Light refreshments can be as small as a fruit tray to as big as a cocktail reception. In either case, there are some refreshments available after the service but it is not a full meal.

Home: Armorbearers do not usually eat at the reception held for guests. They usually escort the guests to the refreshment area and remain in an area near the exit to the room until the guests are ready to leave. Once the guests are ready to leave, they are escorted to the transportation to take them to his hotel accommodations.

On the Road: Even though light refreshments may be available at the engagement site, your pastor may be too tired to participate. If this is the case, liaise with the host Armorbearer to have some of the refreshments packed for the pastor to consume at a later time (If this is his preference). If he does participate in the light refreshments, be sure that he is in your view so that you can mobilize yourself when he is ready to leave.

Prior to leaving the engagement site, find out from the host Armorbearer if there is some place to get a full meal in transit to the hotel in the event that your pastor wants to have a full meal prior to retiring for the night. If he does want to eat, at least you will have an idea of where you can go. In transit to the hotel accommodations, confirm with your pastor whether he wants to have a meal or if he has had enough to eat. If he does, liaise with the driver to see if you can get something from the recommended restaurant or whether there is another place to eat on the way. In either case, be prepared to handle this situation if the need arises.

Once you arrive at the Hotel, escort your pastor to his room and allow him the time and privacy to retire unless otherwise directed.

DINNER

Home: Sometimes when there are guest preachers at your local church, the pastor hosts them to lunch or dinner. When this happens, the Armorbearer should escort the pastor and guest to the room where the meal will be served and then return to the reception where he waits until the meal is completed.

Armorbearers may also be invited to dine, which is usually in an area immediately outside of the dining area. If so, they should remain alert and ensure they are finished eating before the pastor and guests so that they can be in place to receive them after dinner and escort him out of the dining area.

Once the pastor and guests are completed with the meal, the Armorbearer waits at the exit area to receive them from the dining room and escorts them to the transportation that will take the guests to their accommodations. The Armorbearer who is serving the guests should ensure that his garment bags are properly secured and delivered to the transportation when they are ready to leave.

On the Road: If your pastor greets parishioners or attends the product table prior to going to the dining area, you should have a warm towel or hand sanitizer for him to clean his hands en route to the dining room. Also, as you escort your pastor to the dining area, ensure that his hands are free so that he can preserve his energy.

If you are invited to dinner along with your pastor, make a request of the host of the dining room to sit at the opposite end of the table furthest away from your pastor and guest. This will allow him the freedom to discuss private matters without you being in the middle of them. Remember, you are there to serve your pastor, not to socialize with his guests.

While you are present, you can be a resource to the dining host by sharing any dietary concerns or other meal preferences of your pastor with him. For example, if he likes a certain beverage or is allergic to certain foods, ensure that these considerations have been taken into account by the host. You do not want your pastor to have to refuse an item when it is placed before him, because that is not good manners. If you are able to avoid this by simply inquiring ahead of time, that will be of great help to your pastor. If your pastor does have certain preferences for beverages or other items, be sure that you have them with you to make it less of a load on the host church. Also, any medications and other vitamins that are necessary should be on hand for your pastor. Be sure that all of these concerns are noted on the Comfort Assistance Form that should be provided to the host church. A copy of this form is shown in the Appendix.

Ensure that you have completed eating before the host and your pastor wrap up. At the end of the meal, you should be able to escort your pastor to the awaiting transportation after confirming that the garment bag, product materials and other personal effects have been secured in the car. Before you leave, be sure to express thanks on behalf of your pastor and yourself for the hospitality shown to you.

102

B. SERVING IN OTHER WAYS

In this book, we have covered many of the different ways that you can serve your pastor. We have not covered every aspect of every area of service. Your pastor is a unique individual with unique needs, desires and preferences. As an Armorbearer, you should ask your pastor about ways to improve your service. No matter how long you have been serving in this area, there will always be room for improvement because you are changing, the ministry is growing and the demands on your pastor are becoming greater. This means that your role as an Armorbearer is an evolving one. Some things are etched in stone and will not change—you should respect your pastor, have his best interest at heart and be prompt and alert.

Other things are variable and will constantly be changing—whether you make the tea or whether you serve all the time or once a month or whether you travel with the pastor or not. Remain flexible so that you can serve the ministry in the way that is most beneficial to make the vision come alive. To do this, you might have to serve in the background. You may have to serve in obscurity. You may serve the pastor's family but not the pastor directly. In any case, be open to serving your pastor in a way that is most beneficial to him and not necessarily in the traditional way that you have come to understand this role. Remember, one of the main responsibilities of the Armorbearer is to ensure that your pastor is perceived in the best possible light. You must do what you can to make him look good.

C. HELPFUL HINTS FOR THE ARMORBEARER

It takes team work to effectively serve your pastor. Being an Armorbearer is not a one-man or one-woman show. Each Armorbearer is important and he should serve in the place that he has been assigned. Everyone serving in his designated place will ensure that a high level of effectiveness and excellence is maintained. Below are some helpful tips in working in teams if there is more than one Armorbearer assigned to the senior pastor.

- Team work is important—cover one another and do all you can to maintain a cooperative atmosphere.
- Establish a relationship with each other so that you can help each other where necessary. Don't leave each other defenseless.
- Don't laugh when someone makes a mistake—that is a poor reflection on the pastor and indicates that you are not well-trained. Everyone should pitch in to cover each other when something goes wrong. The failure of one person means the failure of the whole team. Work with each other to make sure all areas of serving are being delivered in the spirit of excellence.
- If one of you turns out to be exceptionally efficient, that ought to make you feel proud as a team. Don't develop a bad attitude or become jealous—this hinders the work of the ministry.
- Be a good listener. When people share ministry related problems with you or even personal problems, minister to them. Listen to them and offer whatever support, comfort and help that you are able to give to the situation.
- Be accountable to one another and keep each other from falling. Encourage one another and support one another. Pray for and edify each other. Congratulate each other on a job well done and help to keep each other in good spirits. This improves the service of the ministry as a whole.

- If your spirit is low or you have a bad attitude on any given day, ask the other Armorbearers to pray with you. Don't serve. Ask someone else to cover for you so that you can rejuvenate yourself.

- Be a good follower. One day you will be a leader and you should serve your pastor today the way you would want someone to serve you when you become a leader. If you are not yet at that level, find new and creative ways to improve your service.

CONCLUSION

—ɷ—

W OW! Being an Armorbearer is a lot of work! You better believe that it is, and it takes a serious and anointed person with a call of God on his life to be able to minister to your pastor in an effective way. One of the things I want you to keep foremost in your mind is that this is a spiritual position. Don't be so caught up in serving the man or woman of God and protecting him or her that you do not grow *spiritually*. Prepare yourself so that your sense of discernment will be an asset to your pastor and not a liability. Jonathan's armorbearer is such an example. First Samuel 14:7 says, "So his armorbearer said to him, 'Do all that is in your heart. Go then; here I am with you, according to your heart.'" He was up close to Jonathan but he did not operate in the flesh. The army against Jonathan was more than those with him. In the flesh, his armorbearer would have encouraged him to turn back. The fact that he urged him to do what was in his heart is a testament to the fact that the armorbearer was operating in the spirit and not in the flesh.

I believe that preparation is the key to your success. Proverbs 16:1-3 says,

> *The preparations of the heart belong to man,*
> *But the answer of the tongue is from the LORD.*
> *All the ways of a man are pure in his own eyes,*

But the LORD weighs the spirits.
Commit your works to the LORD,
And your thoughts will be established.

Even though being an Armorbearer is a spiritual job, don't get so "deep" that you forget to prepare yourself to serve. In fact, being an Armorbearer requires personal, emotional, physical, mental and spiritual preparation. We have to prepare ourselves to serve and then dedicate our service to God. If you serve as unto God, you are guaranteed to give excellent service every time.

If you are sure that you are in the right position and on an assignment from God, you had better be prepared for name-calling, struggles and misunderstanding because the devil will seek to distract you and subsequently distract your pastor from sharing the Word of God with the people. This is why you have to be prepared. It is going to be an uphill battle but trust me, it is worth it.

When you were chosen to be an Armorbearer, I know that you were honored! You should be. It is an appointment that should be esteemed highly. The question now is, "Are you ready for your assignment?" With the information contained in this book, I believe that you are ready and prepared to go out and bear the arms of your pastor, so get moving!

I want to admonish you to stay focused, encourage yourself in the Lord, stay faithful to the assignment, and God will give you the desires of your heart. I pray God's blessing on your life and ministry as you undertake this great work. May God empower you as you bear up, lift and support your pastor in the work of the Kingdom.

APPENDIX

—⁓—

THE GARMENTS OF THE BISHOP

—ɯ—

CASSOCK – The medieval cassock, known as the carcalla, was a full-length hooded garment with wide sleeves tightly cuffed at the wrists and usually lined with fur or sheepskin for warmth. It was worn beneath the Alb and was, consequently, unseen. At first it was fastened at the front with ties/strings, but by the thirteenth century buttons were in use, the hood was detachable and the stand collar appeared. Later that century the buttoning became complex and closely spaced and back pleats from waistline to hem were introduced. It is a close-fitting garment, reaching the feet, and may be worn by all ordained clergy as a symbol of a servant. The bishop continues to wear the cassock as part of his garb because Jesus instructed that those who would be chief among to first become servants.

CINCTURE – Material formed in a cumber band like style with the cassock and girded about the waist, serves as a symbol of humility. The scriptures tell us that we must be girded with truth and one such truth is that the minister is first and foremost a humble servant. It obtained its symmetry from the towel which our Lord girded Himself with, as He humbled Himself to wash His disciples' feet. The cincture also symbolizes chastity and purity in thoughts and motives. It also symbolizes having truth encircling your inward being (Ephesians 6:14).

ROCHET – A development of the alb and features very full sleeves, tied into frills at the wrists by bands. It is a ceremonial garment similar to that of a surplice, longer, with sleeve variations and only worn by the bishops. This garment serves as a symbol of the priesthood. It is symbolic of Aaron's white linen ephod, found in the book of Leviticus. The white rochet, worn by the bishop and white surplice, worn by the elders are symbols of the wearer's role as celebrant of the sacraments and chief worship leader among God's people.

CHIMERE – A sleeveless gown usually of red, but sometimes of black material of quality and derived from the Spanish 'Zammarvia' (a twelfth-century riding cloak). It is an upper robe of a bishop. This garment serves as a symbol of the mantle of a prophet. The chimere is only worn by the Bishop because it signifies him as chief proclaimer and defender of the faith in the apostolic tradition. It symbolizes the bishop's role as an apostle, meaning "one who is sent" to travel the world and preach the good news of Jesus Christ.

CROSS – Primarily the instrument of suffering on which Christ died and redeemed the world. It also stands for whatever pain or endurance that a Christian undergoes, and voluntarily accepts, in order to join with Christ and co-operate in the salvation of souls. The cross is, therefore, a revealed mystery, taught by Christ when he said, "If anyone wants to be a follower of mine, let him take up his cross and follow Me (Matt. 16:24).

The mystery of the cross is one of the principal themes of St. Paul's writings to the Romans, Corinthians, Galatians and Philippians. It also represents the victorious risen Savior (different from the crucifix which indicates that He is still on the cross). The pectoral cross is attached to a chain and worn around the neck. The cross hangs on the bishop's breast and thence derives its name, from the Latin *pectas,* the breast. It symbolizes that the bishop is to keep the Cross close to their hearts and remember the love of God in sending His Son to die in order to redeem the world.

GOLD CHAIN – This precious metallic element known as gold is very heavy, malleable and refined. The gold chain is also a symbol of endurance, which emphasizes that the bearer is not a novice. The fold represents deity and wealth. As a gift to the Christ Child, it symbolizes his Kingship. Bishops, only, shall wear the fold chain with the Pectoral Cross. Other appointments shall be issued by Apostolic Order.

RING –The Bishop's ring is an Episcopal ring, like a wedding ring, and symbolizes the Bishop's betrothal to the church and to the people under his or her care. It was a signet ring originally, but is now considered as a symbol of faith or fidelity. It is usually made of gold and set with an amethyst stone.

ZUCHETTO — The small, round skullcap of the ecclesiastic, worn under the berretta. The pope's is white; a cardinal's red; a bishop's purple; a priest's black.

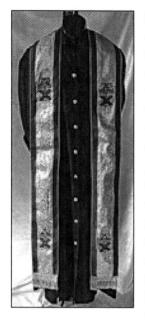

STOLE - A liturgical vestment composed of a strip of material from two to four inches wide and about eighty inches long. It has either a uniform width throughout, or is somewhat narrower towards the middle, widening at the ends in the shape of a trapezium or spade. A small cross is generally sewed or embroidered on the stole at both ends and in the middle; the cross, however, is prescribed only for the middle, where the priest kisses the stole before putting it on. There are no express precepts concerning the material of the stole, but silk, or at least a halfsilk fabric, is most appropriate. Stoles for festivals are generally ornamented with embroidery, especially what are called vesper stoles. The origin of the stole is pre-Christian, but since the sixth century it has been prescribed to be worn by all clergy. In the seventh century, the orarium, or stole, was worn by all ministers celebrating worship services and was worn crossed over the alb, secured in place by the girdle. When worn by a deacon, the modern stole is nearest to its original form, resting on the left shoulder, symbolic of the towel or napkin from which it evolved, and under the right arm, leaving the right side free of encumbrance to attend to sacramental duties. The stole is the symbol of the preacher. It is thinner in width than the tippet.

OTHER GARMENTS USED BY BISHOPS

—ɯɯ—

MITRE– The mitre is a kind of folding cap. It consists of two like parts, each stiffened by a lining and rising to a peak. These are sewn together on the sides but are united above by a piece of material that can fold together. The two points symbolize the Old and New Testaments of which the bishop is teacher. The right to wear the mitre belongs by law only to the pope, the <u>cardinals,</u> and the bishops. The mitre is distinguished from the other Episcopal vestments in that it is always laid aside when the bishop prays. The reason for this is to be found in the commandment of the apostle that a man should pray with uncovered head (1 Corinthians 11:4).

 **STAFF** – The **Episcopal staff** is a symbol of the governing office of the <u>bishop</u> conferred upon ordination. It represents the authority and jurisdiction of the bishop to correct vices, stimulate piety, administer punishment, and govern with a gentleness that is tempered with severity. It is symbolic of prudence and discretion.

MESSAGE CARD

(Used to give messages to the pastor on the pulpit)

BISHOP NEIL C. ELLIS – SENIOR PASTOR/TEACHER

MESSAGE CARD

Bishop Ellis: _____

_____

_____

2006: "Our Year of Victory, Access & Ownership"

Bishop Neil C. Ellis
Senior Pastor/Teacher

MESSAGE CARD

(Used to give messages to the pastor on the pulpit)

—⋙—

PASTOR DELTON D.ELLIS -FIRST ASSISTANT TO THE BISHOP

MESSAGE CARD

Pastor Ellis:

_____

_____

_____

2006: "Our Year of Victory, Access & Ownership"

Bishop Neil C. Ellis
Senior Pastor/Teacher

PASTOR DELTON ELLIS TRAVEL PROFILE

TUESDAY JUNE 20, 2006

—ɷ—

DATE: **Depart Nassau at 1:30 p.m. via US Airways FLT 1234 Arrive in Philadelphia at 4:17 p.m.**

PLACE: **HALLELUJAH BAPTIST CHURCH**
8915 Glory Boulevard
Lindenwood, NJ 088XX
Telephone: 856-721-0000

EVENT: **Pastor's and Layman Power of God Conference**

MINISTRY TIME: **7:30 P.M.**

HOST: **BISHOP DAVID SAINT**

CONTACT: **Rev. Valerie Smith**
Conference Coordinator

HOTEL: **Doubletree Guest Suites**
                         515 Fellowship Road
                         Mt. Laurel, NJ 08054
                         Telephone: 856-778-8999
                         Fax: 856-778-9720
                         Confirmation #: 82127584

DEPARTURE: **Wednesday, June 21, 2006
                         1:35 P.M. US Airways FLT
                         4321 depart Philadelphia
                         5:10 P.M. Arrive in
                         Cleveland**

WEDNESDAY JUNE 21, 2006

DATE: 1:35 P.M. US Airways FLT
                         4321 depart Philadelphia
                         5:10 P.M. Arrive in
                         Cleveland

PLACE: THE GLORY CHURCH
                         3549 Praise Road
                         Cleveland, OH 44826
                         Telephone: 216-741-0000

EVENT: 15TH ANNIVERSARY
                         CONVOCATION

THEME: "FAVOR IS ON US"

MINISTRY TIME: 7:00 P.M.

HOST: BISHOP JOHN MICHAEL

CONTACT: Lisa Major
                         Meeting Planner
                         Telephone: 216-698-0975

HOTEL: Intercontinental
                         9801 Carnegie Ave.
                         Cleveland OH 44106
                         Telephone: 216-707-4300
                         Fax: 216-707-4101
                         Confirmation #: 8218716

DRIVER: **Elder Greg Matthews**

DEPARTURE: Thursday, June 22, 2006
                              8:00 A.M. US Airways FLT
                              8910 depart Cleveland
                              11:10 A.M. Arrive in
                              Nassau

NOTE: YOU WILL BE MET AT THE AIRPORT BY
DEACON JESSE HOLLAND. MOBILE NUMBER:
216-132-4580

TRAVEL CHECKLIST

—〰—

☐ Engagement letter received (outlines nature and scope of engagement)
☐ Phone number and e-mail of contact of engagement host
☐ Vision mission, history, picture of pastor and pastor's family received
☐ Media items (Books/Tapes/CDs/DVDs) are packed
☐ Assistance secured from host church for sale of materials
☐ Serving glass with cover, Gatorade, water, throat lozenges, ginger mints, vitamins, handkerchief, tea bags, honey, hand sanitizer
☐ Medical Items if necessary
☐ Special dietary items if necessary
☐ Passport packed
☐ Ticket received
☐ Per diem received to cover incidental expenses
☐ Retain/Obtain a copy of the sermon or workshop for the pastor's records
☐ Lapelle mic and other ministry aids are available at location
☐ Name and address of host church
☐ Name and phone number of the driver picking up from the airport
☐ Name and address of hotel and confirmation number of reservation

COMFORT ASSISTANCE FORM

Name: _____

Name of ministry: _____

Address:_____

City: _____ State:_____

Phone: _____ Fax:_____ Email:_____

Confirm: date(s) of ministry_____ Time(s) of ministry: _____

Number of persons traveling: _____

Please list their names: _____

_____

Arrival date: _____ Arrival time: _____ Flight No.:_____

Airline: _____ Airport: _____

Departure date: _____ Departure time: _____ Flight No.:_____

Airline: _____ Airport:_____

Do you wish this office to make your travel arrangements?   Yes_____   No_____

Number of rooms required: _____ Room type(s): _____

Hotel preference: _____

Please have hotel information in our office two weeks prior to ministry date.

What you would require: Before speaking: _____

While speaking: _____   After speaking: _____

Will an aide be traveling with you?   Yes_____   No_____

Please list any special needs you might have that may require further assistance (dietary, medical, physical requirements). _____

If you have any other questions or concerns, please contact the Church at:
Telephone: (242) 392-0000 Fax: (242) 392-0000 E-Mail: church@gospel.com

ENGAGEMENT INFORMATION

DATE: _____

CHURCH: _____

PASTOR: _____

PASTOR'S WIFE: _____

OCCASION: _____

SPECIAL GUESTS IN ATTENDANCE:

_____

_____

_____

PRODUCT PROMOTION:

_____

_____

_____

OTHER COMMENTS/OBSERVATIONS:

_____

_____

RECOMMENDED READING

—⟋⟍—

Fasting For Results – Study Guide. Bishop Neil C. Ellis. Legacy Publishers International, Denver CO, 2006. ISBN 1-880809-65-6.

The Art of Armor Bearing: God's Blueprint for Effective Servanthood. Bishop Lester Love. Legacy Publishers International, Denver CO, 2006. ISBN 1-880809-69-9.

A Woman's Guide to Excellence and Elegance. Patrice M. Ellis. Rhema Publishing, Miami FL, 2000. ISBN 0-9679871-4-8.

ABOUT THE AUTHOR

—m—

Pastor Delton Ellis is the First Assistant to Bishop Neil C. Ellis, Senior Pastor of Mount Tabor Full Gospel Baptist Church, the fastest growing church in the Bahamas with a membership of more than 7,000. He is uniquely qualified for this assignment having served in virtually every capacity of church leadership ranging from Sunday school teacher, to Youth Director to his current post as First Assistant giving oversight to 45 members of staff and a 250 member volunteer team. He has served in all areas of the Ministry of HELPS, and is a Mentor to many who operate in these callings today.

Pastor Delton Ellis is the CEO of **Keepers of the Temple Ministries International**, a ministry dedicated to helping Pastors and other Leaders to develop a training regimen that will ensure that those who serve in ministry do so with a spirit of excellence. Pastor Ellis' special understanding of **service** has been harnessed during the ten years he served as Quality Control Manager for two of the largest fast food chains in the Bahamas, his previous appointments as Chairman and Vice President of two of the local School Boards in Nassau, Bahamas and currently as a Director of the National Insurance Board of the Bahamas and as First Assistant at Mount Tabor. Serving in these capacities has allowed Pastor Ellis to develop the gift the Lord has given him and today, the Kingdom is the beneficiary of a mature and established recipe for developing the proper attitudes and skills for success in Ministry. Through his experience and unique insight, he is able to make the difficult challenge of serving others something that can be easily put into practice. His love for people and for serving only complements this experience.

Pastor Ellis holds Certificates from the **Institute for Thinking Development** (*Creative Thinking*), **The Possibility Institute of John Maxwell** (*The Laws of Leadership*), **The University of Miami School of Business Administration Executive Education Program** (*Creative Thinking and Innovative Strategy)* and the **Trinity School of Continuing Studies** (*Premarital Counseling*). He is a member of the *Religious Conference Management Association* (RCMA) and the *Atlantis Priority Club.* He is the author of 4 books; **Developing a Heart for Service** (textbook and workbook) and **How to Make Your Dream Come Alive** (textbook and workbook) and has conducted numerous Workshops and Seminars on **Ministry of Helps** and **Leadership** both in the Bahamas and Internationally. Pastor Ellis is the President of Frontline Investment Club and the Issachar Investment Club and is a Justice of the Peace (JP) in the Commonwealth of the Bahamas.

Pastor Ellis and his beautiful wife Anna, live in Nassau, Bahamas with their three daughters Delnika, Dalanna and Deandra.

OTHER BOOKS BY
THE AUTHOR

—ɯ—

In his first book _Developing a Heart for Service_, Pastor Ellis explains what the Ministry of HELPS is, what it does and the kind of 'helpers' that should be involved in it. The book is a step by step guide to starting a Ministry of HELPS for those ministries that do not have one and providing the tools to strengthen already existing HELPS ministries. Everything from identifying the needs of your ministry, developing a Spirit of Excellence, testing the Spirit of Helpers to knowing what to do and what to wear are covered in this work.

The workbook that accompanies this text serves to reinforce the principles outlined in the book. If you have been called to serve as a _Parking Lot Attendant, Outside Greeter, Door Greeter, Hospitality Worker, Usher, Protocol Officer, Armor Bearer, Deacon, Minister, Elder_ or _Associate Pastor_, reading this book is a MUST.

"Pastor Delton Ellis has been learning and successfully developing while applying a unique gift of servitude to the Body of Christ and his Senior Pastor Bishop Neil C. Ellis. Delton Ellis has a heart for service and he personifies the grace of humility in service for the 21st Century Church. I am delighted that he has shared his wealth of knowledge and experiences in this form, as a contemporary reference for you as servant-gifts to Pastors and ministries throughout the Body of Christ."

Ed Watson
Senior Pastor, Trinity Assembly, Nassau, Bahamas

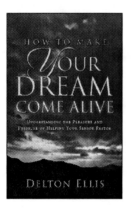

In this book, <u>How to Make Your Dream Come Alive</u>, Pastor Ellis addresses a critical and frequently challenged aspect of God's work - that of serving your Leader by helping them to make their vision come to pass. It is almost counterintuitive to most people whose first priority is accomplishing their own dream. This is not God's way to success. In this book, Pastor Ellis explains how, as servants and helpers, our dream comes to pass while we help our Leaders' dream to materialize. In explaining the process for progress, the book provides practical information on how we can help our leader and protect ourselves from the dangers we will face along the way. It highlights the perspective, the attitude, the focus, the commitment and the patience that must be developed if we are to be successful in making our own dreams come alive.

The workbook that accompanies this text serves to reinforce the principles outlined in the book.

"When the name Delton Ellis is mentioned, there are at least three words that leap into my spirit. These words are Service, Protocol and Leadership. When one is in his presence, these unique qualities ensue from him in a practical and overwhelming way. One encounter with this rare gift to the body of Christ in any capacity – as an author, conference speaker, preacher or workshop presenter will confirm and demonstrate the aforementioned qualities. The insights in this book will not only provide valuable information and inspiration but if embraced, will increase your level of excellence and influence."

The Right Reverend Dr. Paul C. Cockfield
Senior Pastor, Battallion Pentecostal Assembly Averne,
New York

PRODUCTS AND SERVICES

	Keepers of the Temple Ministries International

WORKSHOPS AND SEMINARS:

- Vision
- Commitment
- Leadership
- Armorbearers & Protocol Officers
- Greeters, Hospitality Workers & Ushers
- Ministry of HELPS

SERVICES:

- Conference/Event Planning
- Conference/Event Hosting
- Concierge/VIP Services

SERMONS:

- I Came Prepared to Worship
- Please Cover the Back Door
- A Major Sacrifice: I'm a Passionate Worshipper Too
- Why Are You Still There?
- When Helping Them is Helping Me
- And many more….

Please visit our website at www.keepersofthetemple.com for more information.

Preparing Others to Serve with a Spirit of Excellence
Through Information, Observation and Transformation.

Willow Tree Avenue and Mount Tabor Drive
P.O. Box N-9705 Nassau, Bahamas

ORDER FORM

NAME: _____

ADDRESS: _____

CITY: _____ STATE: _____ ZIP: _____

P.O. BOX: _____ EMAIL ADDRESS: _____

PHONE: (HM) _____ (WK) _____ (MOBILE) _____

BOOK TITLE(S): _____

_____

SERMON TITLE(S): _____

_____

WORKSHOP/SEMINAR TITLE(S): _____

_____

METHOD OF PAYMENT: (Please tick)

Cash   Cheque   Money Order   VISA

NAME OF CREDIT CARD HOLDER: _____

CREDIT CARD NUMBER: _____ EXP DATE: _____

SIGNATURE: _____

If you have any questions, please contact us;
(242) 392- 0377 *(Phone)*
(242) 392-2767 *(Fax)*
keepersofthetemple@yahoo.com *(Email)*

CONTACT INFORMATION

—ɯ—

To order one of the books or sermons offered by Keepers of the Temple Ministries International, please visit the **Online Store** at www.keepersofthetemple.com.

To schedule Pastor Ellis for a Seminar or Workshop or to engage another service of Keepers of the Temple Ministries International, please contact us at the address below. Keepers of the Temple stands ready to assist you to give you the tools you need to complete your God-given assignment.

KEEPERS OF THE TEMPLE MINISTRIES INTERNATIONAL

Willowtree Avenue and Mount Tabor Drive
Pinewood Gardens
P.O. Box N-9705
Nassau, Bahamas

Phone: (242) 392-0377
Fax: (242) 392-2767

Email: keepersofthetemple@yahoo.com
Wesbsite: www.keepersofthetemple.com

ACKNOWLEDGEMENTS

—ɷ—

There are very few people that I have had the opportunity to encounter that have a grasp for excellence in the area of Armour-bearing and the Ministry of Helps. Pastor Delton Ellis has more than a theoretical knowledge of these ministries, but has the practical experience and spiritual development to accompany the knowledge. In my mind, he is a consummate example of what God talks about when He says, "You shall know them by their fruit." I highly recommend Pastor Delton's book to any church, group or organization that wants a God oriented ministry tool on how to support the man or woman of God.

Bishop George W. Brooks
Bishop of Administration
Full Gospel Baptist Fellowship International
Senior Pastor, Mount Zion Baptist Church
Greensboro, North Carolina

To the hardest working man I know. I want to say congratulations on a job well done. This book will be an inspiration first to Hundreds, then to Thousands, then to Millions. The knowledge imparted in this book will cause every

Armorbearer to successfully fulfill the call of God on their life as they serve the Senior Pastor.

Bishop Kevin V. Gresham, Sr.
Senior Pastor, Greater Saint John Church
Upper Marlborough, Maryland

Pastor Delton Ellis is the consummate Armorbearer and will make any Leader look good. In this 21st Century where everybody is just caught up in positions and going after "Titles" here is a book that says you can serve others and still advance the Kingdom. The Body of Christ is privileged to have him share his anointed insight into what God seeks to do through this valuable Ministry.

Bishop Arnold Josey
Senior Pastor, Commonwealth Mission Baptist Church
Nassau, Bahamas

ACKNOWLEDGEMENTS

—ⱳ—

Pastor Delton Ellis is a gift from God to the Body of Christ. The mantle of servitude on his life can only be manifested through the anointing of humility that he so easily displays. It takes an anointing and a mantle to share what Pastor Ellis shares with the Body of Christ. If your Helps Ministry is to flow in the Spirit of Excellence, you must receive what he has to offer.

District Overseer Frederick Hardy
Senior Pastor, Faith Full Gospel Baptist Church
Montgomery, Alabama

Pastor Delton Ellis is a tremendous blessing to the Body of Christ, both locally and internationally, and has most certainly been a blessing to Living Waters Kingdom Ministries as he continues to serve as an Armorbearer. Over the years, I have found him to be a humble servant of God, willing and ready to help and support. Particularly, I have watched his service to Bishop Neil C. Ellis, and have found it to be impeccable and commendable. Personally, I see Pastor Delton Ellis as a 21st Century Elisha, one that faithfully serves. I am certain that this book will be a blessing to Pastors, Leaders, Armorbearers and their ministry as they read it. Congratulations on your new venture, as you continue to fulfill the vision that God has given you.

Apostle Raymond Wells
Senior Pastor, Living Waters Kingdom Ministries
Nassau, Bahamas

Pastor Delton Ellis is a nationally recognized and celebrated business owner with a passion for building the Kingdom of God and sharing a message of service and protocol to every person who has a dream to follow and do God's best. This servanthood is exemplified in his capacity as First Assistant to Bishop Neil C. Ellis, Senior Pastor of Mount Tabor Full Gospel Baptist Church in Nassau Bahamas. I know that this book will be a tremendously blessing to all who will read it and apply its principles to their service in Ministry.

Linda Thompson
Elder – Mount Tabor Full Gospel Baptist Church
Senior Manager, Airlift and Reception Services
Bahamas Ministry of Tourism

Printed in the United States
81130LV00002B/1-195

9 781600 345739